IDEAS ON TRIAL

ELIZABETH BLACKWELL

FIRST WOMAN DOCTOR
OF MODERN TIMES

Adele Glimm

JB
BLACKWELL

McGraw-Hill

New York St. Louis San Francisco Auckland Bogotá Caracas
Lisbon London Madrid Mexico City Milan Montreal
New Delhi San Juan Singapore Sydney Tokyo Toronto

A Bank Street Biography

To Zoe, Laura, and Annabel,
who can be anything they want to be

Ideas on Trial

The *Ideas on Trial* series presents dramatic stories of men and women in science and medicine who waged heroic struggles and risked their comfort, freedom, reputations, and sometimes their lives, for the sake of pursuing their work.

The authors use a docu-drama, "you are there" style to tell these exciting stories. Wherever possible, actual reported scenes and dialog are used, along with quotes from letters, diaries, newspapers, and journals of the time. In a few cases, however, the authors had to invent scenes and dialog for events that did occur, but for which there was no reported scene or dialog.

---

1 2 3 4 5 6 7 8 9 0 DOC/DOC 0 9 8 7 6 5 4 3 2 1 0

ISBN 0-07-134335-0

The Bank Street Series Project Editor was Elisabeth Jakab.

The sponsoring editor for this book was Griffin Hansbury, the editing supervisor was Maureen B. Walker, and the production supervisor was Charles H. Annis. The cover and text were designed and set in New Century Schoolbook by Marsha Cohen/ Parallelogram Graphics.

McGraw-Hill books are available at special quantity discounts to use as premiums and sales promotions, or for use in corporate training programs. For more information, please write to the Director of Special Sales, McGraw-Hill, Two Penn Plaza, New York, NY, 10121-2298.

CONTENTS

Elizabeth Blackwell. (The Schlesinger Library, Radcliffe Institute, Harvard University.)

1

THE FIRST STEP ON A LONG JOURNEY

On the wind-whipped morning of November 7, 1847, Elizabeth Blackwell hurried down the hallway after the Dean, Dr. Charles Alfred Lee, who was leading her to her first class at Geneva Medical College. Through the hallway window she saw bare tree branches bending and dipping and the rain lashing the school grounds. But the storm outside seemed calm to Elizabeth compared to the storm she could hear through the closed door when Dr. Lee stopped outside the classroom.

Students were laughing and shouting, though she could not make out any words. It sounded as if books were being thrown and chairs were crashing to the floor. She did not have to see the students to know that every last one of them was male. There had never been a woman medical student at this college in New York State. Never until today.

Dr. Lee looked almost as nervous as Elizabeth felt. "Miss Blackwell, I do not know how the other students will receive you. Many of them are rather rough young fellows in their manners. Even on ordinary days we teachers have difficulty controlling their behavior and today –"

Elizabeth was twenty-six years old but she felt as if she were a little girl again, wondering if boys would throw snowballs at her. *What does he mean? Will the students throw things at me, run me out of class? Will they make me wish I'd never been admitted?* Aloud she said, "Dr. Lee, I'm sure I can put up with whatever happens."

More shouts and crashing noises came through the classroom door. Until this moment, Elizabeth had felt that being admitted to medical school was the most wonderful

Geneva Medical College, 1848. (Courtesy, Geneva Historical Society, New York.)

thing that had ever happened to her. Twenty-eight medical schools had rejected her. None of them would consider allowing a woman to study medicine. At last Geneva, the twenty-ninth school, sent her a letter of admission.

"I believe it must be time for class to begin," Elizabeth said, amazing herself by at least *sounding* confident. "Should we not go in?"

Dr. Lee smiled weakly. "They can hardly start without me, since I am the teacher." He looked as if he would rather run and hide than face his students today. But he opened the classroom door.

Now Elizabeth could hear some of what the students were shouting: "Hey, those girls next door won't even look at us!" "Where's that woman student *we're* supposed to have?" "Watch it, here's Lee!"

"If you would wait here, Miss Blackwell," Dr. Lee said loudly above the noise, "I will prepare them for your presence today." Then he went into the classroom, shutting the door behind him.

As soon as Dr. Lee entered, the students dashed for their desks. Feet pounded, chairs scraped against the floor. Dr. Lee cleared his throat. When he began to speak, his voice shook. "Gentlemen, I have an important announcement."

From the back of the room, a loud voice said, "Yeah, the town's shutting us down—too rowdy!"

Whistles and loud laughter drowned out Dr. Lee as he tried to continue. At last he succeeded. "You remember that the faculty asked you to decide about a certain application. You voted to admit the applicant, who has arrived – "

A rumble of excited voices: "Where is she? We want a look at her!"

Dr. Lee raised his voice. "I don't have to tell you how to behave – "

"Then don't tell us!" someone shouted.

" – behave to a lady!" Dr. Lee himself was almost shouting now.

"A lady! Thought she wanted to be a doctor!"

Shaking his head, Dr. Lee went to the door and opened it. *Well, this whole business was not my idea,* he thought.

When Elizabeth saw the look on his face, she was more afraid than ever. Then she straightened up, lifting her chin. She had worked so hard, and against so much opposition! She was not going to turn back now. Looking neither to the left nor the right she walked calmly into the classroom.

There was total silence as Dr. Lee escorted Elizabeth across the room. He placed a chair for her near his desk. "Gentlemen, may I present your fellow student, Miss Elizabeth Blackwell."

Elizabeth did not once glance at the other students, but she was intensely aware of their stares. What had they expected of a woman medical student? She wondered if they were surprised that she was small and thin and dressed plainly in a Quaker-gray gown. She removed her simple gray bonnet, put it under her chair, sat down, and opened her notebook.

Dr. Lee began his lecture.

Elizabeth looked only up at Dr. Lee and down at her notebook. She wrote industriously. But she did not hear any

Learning to be a medical doctor, c. 1850. (Culver Pictures.)

other notebook pages turning or any other pens scraping on paper. The only sound was Dr. Lee's voice. She was sure the students were simply continuing to stare at her, not taking notes at all. *Well, I'm learning medicine. Let them waste their time if they want to.*

Elizabeth's Impact

Here is how Stephen Smith, a fellow student who was to become a well-known physician, recorded Elizabeth's arrival: "A hush fell over the class as if each member had been stricken by paralysis.... A death-like stillness prevailed during the lecture.... It is quite impossible to magnify the power of the personality of Miss Blackwell over the lawless elements of that class.... Though there were disorder and disturbance in her absence, as before her admission, yet the moment that she entered upon the platform the most perfect order and quiet prevailed." The *Boston Medical Journal* described her in these words: "...a pretty little specimen of the feminine gender...comes into the class with great composure...."

Elizabeth was right. The students were paralyzed with amazement. This woman student was no aggressive Amazon. Nor did she seem to be a "bad" woman, for no bad woman would dress so modestly and plainly. She seemed to be very much a lady and she was rather pretty, too.

When Dr. Lee announced that the lecture was over, Elizabeth grew nervous again. Would they all dash over and surround her chair? Would they follow her from the room, making rude remarks, brushing up against her? But no one moved. Like perfect gentlemen, the other students waited for Elizabeth to gather up her things and leave first.

Out in the hallway, Elizabeth felt as if her whole life had changed since she had waited out here for Dr. Lee to introduce her. The worst was over. Now she was really a medical student.

Wondering what her next class would be like, she thought, *thank you, Papa, for giving me the same education as my brothers so I'm used to learning alongside boys.* She remembered how surprised the new governess, Miss Major, had been when she discovered what it would be like to teach Samuel Blackwell's daughters. How sad Papa had not lived to see where Elizabeth's education had led her!

Four more lectures to go today. But now I know I can do it.

CHAPTER 2

THE UNUSUAL EDUCATION OF THE BLACKWELL DAUGHTERS

Nine-year-old Elizabeth Blackwell peered over the top of her geography book at the young woman talking to her father in the doorway of their home schoolroom. *Oh please be our teacher!* she thought.

Elizabeth's sister Anna, thirteen, sitting next to her at the table, nudged her. "Stop staring, Elizabeth," Anna said in a low voice. "It's rude."

Immediately, Elizabeth dropped her eyes to the map of England on the page before her. Anna was right, it wasn't polite to stare. But she had to see what the new governess was like. That wasn't really staring, was it? She was *admiring* Miss Major, who was so pretty and had such a kind smile. Not a bit like Aunt Barbara, Papa's sister, who lived with the family and had been teaching the children until now.

Aunt Bar, as her nieces and nephews called her, never smiled and she never seemed to think Elizabeth did anything right, no matter how hard she tried. Aunt Bar kept a little Black Book, in which she wrote down everything the children did wrong. Somehow Elizabeth's name found its way into the Black Book more often than that of any of her seven brothers and sisters.

"What do you think, Miss Major?" Samuel Blackwell asked. "Would you enjoy teaching my sons and daughters?"

Eliza Major smiled at the five children working at lessons around the big table. They seemed to be well behaved. It would not be difficult to teach them, especially since the older three were girls. What did girls learn, after all? Music, sketching, embroidery, some simple French.

The smallest girl was stealing glances at her. "What is your name, my dear?" Miss Major asked, smiling at the thin child with the straight, pale hair and the serious expression.

"Elizabeth Blackwell, ma'am."

"And what are you studying today, Elizabeth?"

"Latin and geography this afternoon," Elizabeth answered. "This morning we had a mathematics lesson."

Miss Major choked back her surprise. Latin and mathematics, indeed! What an odd family. The two older girls must be more advanced in their studies. Did she, Eliza, know enough to keep up with them?

Samuel Blackwell repeated his question. "Would you like to teach my children?"

Miss Major hesitated. As a single woman, she had to earn her own living. Teaching was almost the only work open to a respectable lady. "Yes, Mr. Blackwell, I would. I can see that your children are hard working and well brought up. But – is it not a little unusual to teach girls such subjects?"

"My daughters have good minds," Mr. Blackwell said. "Good minds should have good training. Who knows what my daughters may do in life?"

Miss Major was amazed. She thought, *he speaks as if there is a wide choice of things they CAN do!*

With the question of her employment settled, Mr. Blackwell invited her to get to know her new pupils. Moving around the table, she spoke to each child in turn. Anna, next to Elizabeth, had dark curly hair and seemed a very confident young lady. Next came quiet Marian, delicate looking and ten years old. Six-year-old Samuel told her proudly that he could read but that his little brother Henry was just learning the alphabet.

From the next room, Eliza Major heard the gentle voice of the children's mother speaking to her younger children. Mr. Blackwell had told her there were three little ones who would be her pupils when they grew big enough. A baby cried and Mrs. Blackwell began to sing a lullaby. Eliza felt herself relax. She would like being part of this family.

Miss Major had come around to Elizabeth once more. "Will you give us *hard* work to do?" Elizabeth asked shyly.

"Oh no, not too hard, Elizabeth. You mustn't worry."

Elizabeth thought, *but I want to do hard work!* She didn't say so, though, for that might be bragging.

In the days that followed, Elizabeth was overjoyed to have a real teacher, and she was sure she was learning

Elizabeth Blackwell at age eleven. (Archives and Special Collections on Women in Medicine. MCP Hahnemann University, Phildelphia.)

more. She didn't get into trouble with Miss Major as she had with Aunt Bar.

Of the four Blackwell aunts who lived with the family, it was Aunt Bar who was in charge of the older children. One night, checking on the children, Aunt Bar found Elizabeth wrapped in her quilt, curled up on the floor of the room she shared with Marian. "What is the meaning of this, child?"

"My bed is too comfortable," Elizabeth said. "I want to find out if I can do hard things."

"What nonsense will you think up next! Get into bed at once!"

Elizabeth was sure there would be a punishment for going to bed without a bed, though she didn't see why it should matter to anyone but her. *When I'm grown, I will do exactly what I want and no one will stop me,* she thought.

But she didn't stop trying to test herself. The next day, she sat quietly through dinner, eating very little. Toward the end of the meal she said politely, "No pudding for me, please, Mama."

"But blackberry pudding is your favorite!" Mama said, her big silver spoon suspended over the pudding bowl. "Are you feeling ill, Elizabeth?"

"Bed and medicine for her," Aunt Bar said darkly, shaking her head. And she added, "That child should be thankful to be offered pudding."

Next to Elizabeth, Anna whispered, "You're not ill. I know what you're doing, Elizabeth. You're trying to see if you can do without things."

Elizabeth didn't answer. She wanted that pudding so much she could have reached out and grabbed Anna's portion. But how would she ever know if she could do difficult things if she didn't try?

Mama said Elizabeth didn't have to go to bed early, in spite of not eating pudding. After dinner the whole family gathered around the fire in the parlor while Papa read aloud. Mama and Aunt Bar sewed or embroidered while they listened and Miss Major corrected the children's schoolwork.

Tonight's book was a collection of religious stories. Elizabeth sat closest to Papa, lifting her tiny sister Ellen up so she could see the pictures. The stories could be a little boring but the pictures were wonderful: woods, streams, and waterfalls.

Elizabeth felt so safe with her whole family around her and Papa's strong voice in her ears. But at the same time she was thinking: *I want to grow up and see the world and do exciting things.*

As Papa read, Elizabeth noticed that Miss Major sometimes sniffed delicately at the air as if she were puzzled by some odor but was trying not to be rude. *She's not used to the sugar smell yet,* Elizabeth thought.

Later, just before the older girls were sent up to bed, Elizabeth and Anna met with Miss Major in the schoolroom so she could return the essays they had written that morning. It was a chance to explain the mysterious smell. "It's from Papa's sugar refinery," Elizabeth said.

Anna explained, "Papa's work is taking sugar cane, a plant that grows in warm countries, and turning it into the sugar we put in our tea. It's better for Papa to live near his business, so the sugar refinery is next door." Then Anna sighed. "But the rest of us have to live with that smell," she complained. "I can't bear it!"

"I don't mind it," Elizabeth said.

"I certainly won't mind it," Miss Major said. "As long as I like sugar in my tea, I can hardly object to a sugar refinery."

"It isn't the smell that matters about sugar," Elizabeth went on. "It makes Papa sad to be in the sugar business because the sugar cane is grown by slaves. Papa thinks it's wrong for any people to be owned by other people. I think so, too."

"There's no slavery in England," Miss Major said gently. "And we can pray that someday there won't be slavery in England's colonies or anywhere else."

Elizabeth knew that Papa did pray for the end of slavery, for every morning he led them in prayers before breakfast. She also knew that he went to meetings with men called "abolitionists" because they were determined to abolish, or end, slavery by getting governments to outlaw it everywhere.

Often these meetings were held in the Blackwell house, Elizabeth told Miss Major. "You children are lucky to meet such people," Miss Major said. "They are doing important work in the world."

"When I grow up," Elizabeth announced, "I will do important work." Then she paused, feeling a little unsure of herself. "I just don't know what it will be."

CHAPTER 3

FIRE, RIOTS, CHOLERA, AND SAILING TO AMERICA

On the morning of October 29, 1831, ten-year-old Elizabeth and her two older sisters left their rented house in the country, where the family lived from spring until winter set in. The girls were going to Bristol where the Blackwell home was, which they did on the days they had drawing lessons. They piled into the yellow carriage with Papa; then Bessie Gray the pony began to pull the carriage. Elizabeth, Anna, and Marian waved good-bye to Mama and their younger sisters and brothers.

But when they reached a toll gate, the gatekeeper warned them that mobs were rioting in Bristol. "See that red glow in the sky?" the gatekeeper said excitedly. "They're setting fires everywhere."

Papa was very upset. "I must get to the sugar refinery before they burn it down!" he said. "And to the center of town to try to help calm things down. But first I'll take you girls back to Mama where you'll be safe."

"No, Papa, we're going with you!" Elizabeth cried.

"Your safety is more important than lessons," Papa said sternly.

Elizabeth looked him in the eye. "We have to go with *you*, Papa," she said. She could tell that he understood it was not the drawing lessons that mattered. Rather, his daughters could not imagine letting him go alone into whatever dangers threatened.

When they reached Bristol, Papa left them at their house, cautioning them to stay inside with the doors locked. Then he was gone.

The girls were terrified that he would be hurt, maybe even killed. All day, Anna and Marian paced up and down the rooms of the house, afraid to look out the windows. Only Elizabeth kept watch at the drawing room window, where she could see smoke and flames in the distance. *Please make Papa be safe,* she prayed as she watched. And then, hoping she was not asking too much, she added, *and please don't let them burn down the sugar refinery.*

It was two o'clock the next morning before Papa came home. The girls, who had been too worried to sleep, surrounded him, hugging him hard. His coat was covered with ashes and smelled of smoke, but he was back and he was safe. Elizabeth thought of Mama. How worried she must be because they had not come back that evening! If only they could let her know they were all right!

"The sugar refinery, Papa," Elizabeth said. "Is it...?"

"It is still standing," Papa said grimly.

"Why did the people riot, Papa?" Marian asked, when Papa had had a chance to rest.

"They want better working conditions, the right to vote. But violence is never the way to change anything."

Later, Papa's friend Mr. Goodwin told the family how Papa and two other men had stood in front of St. Mary Redcliffe church to protect it from the angry mob. "Blackwell and the others were extremely brave," Mr. Goodwin said. "The mob might have killed them." And he went on to tell them that two hundred years ago, Queen Elizabeth had called St. Mary Redcliffe the most beautiful church in all of England.

Elizabeth was proud of her father but she cared more for his safety than for all the beautiful churches in the world.

The riots (to be known as the Bristol Riots) were not the only major problem to strike the Blackwells' home city that year. There was an outbreak of the dreaded disease cholera and some people had already died of it.

One evening, not long after the riots, Papa surprised them by announcing at the end of dinner: "I will not read to you tonight. Instead, Mama and I have something important to tell all of you. Let us gather near the fire." Surprised, the children began to follow the adults to the parlor.

Elizabeth hung back, whispering to her brother Sam: "Papa looks so tired and worried. What can be happening?"

"Poor Papa has lost a lot of money," Sam answered in a low voice. "The sugar business is very bad now."

Elizabeth was impressed that Sam, even younger than

she, knew about such things. When she said this to him, he answered, "Girls and women are not supposed to know about money and business. Only we men do."

Elizabeth knew Sam didn't mean to hurt her feelings. But she thought, *between the things girls aren't supposed to know and the things children aren't supposed to know, it's a wonder I know anything!* Then she told herself, *when I grow up, I will know everything about the world that I want to know.*

A few moments later, Papa's announcement drove this thought from her head. "Mama and I have decided that we will leave England and sail to America. We will start a new life. I am convinced I will be able to earn a better living for our family there."

Elizabeth was both amazed and excited. Moving to a foreign country! What would it be like there? Good or bad, at least she would see the world! But she noticed that Mama looked very sad. *Mama doesn't want to go,* she thought, *but she's letting Papa decide.*

Marian was the first to speak. "Are people dying of cholera in America the way they are here, Papa?" she asked.

Mama said quickly: "Don't frighten the children, Marian. You know Papa will take care of us wherever we are."

The ship the Blackwells boarded in August 1832 was called the *Cosmo.* "There are so many of us, will we take up the whole ship?" little Henry asked as their carriage neared the pier.

Papa laughed. "The ship can hold hundreds of people, Henry. Last time I counted, there were only sixteen of us."

*Immigrants arrive in New York, as the Blackwells did after their
journey from England in 1832. (Culver Pictures.)*

Besides Papa and Mama and eight children, there were
three aunts (one aunt decided to stay in England), two
maids, and Eliza Major, the governess.

Right away, Elizabeth and Anna knew that something
was wrong with the ship's cabin they were to share with
several other girls. In the center of it was an iron pipe,
which was leaking. "Ugh, what is that horrible smell?"
Elizabeth asked, whisking her skirts away from the area of
the pipe.

"It's a sewage drainpipe!" Anna cried, holding her nose.
"How disgusting!" The sewage pipe continued to leak and

several times each day, Anna would exclaim: "How can people live this way?"

When they told Papa about the pipe, he told them that most of the people on board lived in conditions that were much worse. More than two hundred people were traveling steerage, he said, which meant they all lived crowded together on a dark lower deck with no private cabins at all.

The pipe was not the worst trial for Elizabeth during the voyage. She was so seasick that for much of the trip she could barely hold her head up and could eat almost nothing. When she did eat, she often threw up soon afterward. Then she was afraid she smelled even worse than the leaking pipe!

Even if she hadn't been seasick, the food on board was not very tempting. Early in the voyage a cow on board provided milk. But the cow soon died. After that, their only food was salted meat and crackers.

One morning, Anna and Elizabeth were out walking on the deck for exercise. Usually they walked only along one side of the ship and back. But the sea was calmer than usual, so Elizabeth was feeling less seasick and more eager to explore. Rounding a corner onto the back deck, the girls looked down and saw two sailors heaving a long canvas bundle over the rail into the sea. "What can they be doing?" Anna asked.

Elizabeth was gripped by a sudden cold fear. She knew at once what they were doing. "It's a body," she whispered, guessing why death had touched their ship: cholera had followed them from England. Mama said that Papa would take care of them wherever they were, but Elizabeth knew Papa could do nothing against the horror of cholera.

One sailor looked up and saw the two young girls watching. "You shouldn't be here," he called out. "What are you doing?"

Anna was too upset to answer but Elizabeth said, "It's cholera, isn't it?"

How Cholera Claims Its Victims

Cholera is caused by bacteria usually found in unclean food or water, which enter the body through the mouth. The body becomes dehydrated (dried out through loss of fluids) due to diarrhea and vomiting. This results in a dangerous loss of necessary minerals like salt and potassium. If cholera is not treated, about 60 percent of its victims die, as they did in Elizabeth's time when effective treatment was unknown. Modern-day treatment involves replacing fluids and salt and giving antibiotics.

The first major advance in controlling the disease came in 1854 when a British doctor, John Snow, discovered that a contaminated water pump in London was the source of the bacteria that led to a cholera epidemic.

The sailor hesitated and she expected him to reply that girls weren't supposed to know anything about it. But instead he nodded. "Count yourselves lucky to be traveling up there where there's no disease. Many are sick down below."

After that, Anna never again asked how people could expect to live with a leaking, smelly drainpipe.

But Elizabeth asked, again and again: "Why do people have to die of cholera? Can't doctors do something?"

CHOLERA IN TODAY'S WORLD

➤ Today cholera mostly occurs among people living in poverty in tropical and subtropical regions with poor sanitation. The drainpipe that leaked sewage was the kind of unsanitary situation that might have allowed cholera germs to spread and infect people. One of Elizabeth's major contributions after she became a doctor was to teach people that cleanliness, such as simple handwashing and keeping flies away from food, was an effective way of avoiding disease.

4

MORE CHOLERA, ABOLITIONISTS, THE GREAT FIRE OF 1835, AND A RUNAWAY SLAVE

The voyage to America took so long – seven weeks and four days – that Elizabeth felt she would be living on the *Cosmo*, smelling the sewage pipe, and throwing up forever. But at last, in October 1832, the ship docked in New York. *A new country! A new city! And no more seasickness!* The first thing Elizabeth was aware of as she stepped off the ship was how solid the ground felt beneath her feet. The next thing was how empty New York seemed. Wasn't it supposed to be a big, busy city? It was so quiet she could hear the footsteps of her family on the cobblestones.

The Blackwells were dressed in their best clothes to meet their new country but there were scarcely any people on the streets to see the three older girls in their slate blue cloaks and bonnets or their father in his tan greatcoat and tall beaver hat. "We will walk to our hotel," Papa told his family, after arranging with porters to transport their baggage in wheelbarrows.

"I thought there would be crowds in New York," Marian said.

"We're a crowd all by ourselves," Elizabeth answered as sixteen of them moved slowly along the quiet streets. She wondered why all the windows were shuttered in the buildings they passed.

"I smell fresh bread!" Henry cried suddenly. He and Sam ran ahead, guided by their noses to the open door of a bakery. When Papa reached them, he and the boys went inside, returning a few minutes later with the first fresh bread the family had tasted in many weeks.

But Papa looked very grave. "The baker says there is a cholera epidemic here. People have either gone to the country to escape the disease or are staying shut up at home." *So that explains the ghostly quiet, the windows with their shutters closed*, Elizabeth thought.

The house Papa rented on Thompson Street a few days later was tall and narrow, with the kitchen in the basement and the other rooms piled on top of each other. Coming downstairs to breakfast on the first morning in their new home, Elizabeth whispered to Anna: "It feels like a cage! The walls are too close."

But it was the cholera that really made the children feel caged. Marian grumbled, "We might as well have stayed in Bristol if there was going to be cholera."

Elizabeth answered, "Someday someone will figure out why people die of cholera and maybe it won't happen so much anymore." Luckily, the Blackwells themselves stayed healthy, as they had in Bristol and on the ship.

Only a few weeks after they reached America, a new brother was born. He was named George Washington Blackwell and was the only one of the family to be a native-born American.

At last, the cholera epidemic died out. The children began exploring their new city, beginning with their own neighborhood, called Greenwich Village, where they sometimes saw pigs roaming the streets. They went farther afield as they grew used to New York. Papa took them to see Wall Street with its bankers and stockbrokers, the museums, the wholesale markets where storekeepers bought groceries for their shops, and the dealers in furs, leather, and silks. And just as they had in England, the Blackwell girls had the same opportunities to learn from the city that their brothers did.

Meanwhile, Papa was busy with his new sugar refinery. He was also becoming deeply involved with the American anti-slavery movement, which got him into trouble with other men in the sugar business. "Blackwell, without slaves to grow the sugar we'd all starve!" they told him, growing angrier the more he talked about how evil it was for men to own their fellow human beings.

Papa did more than just talk: he lived his beliefs. He offered their home as a refuge for the Cox family (a father, mother, and five children). Mr. Cox was a preacher and abolitionist and had been threatened with death by some anti-abolitionists (people who were against outlawing or abolishing slavery). Then his brother, a doctor in danger for the same reason, also moved in.

For three weeks, the already crowded Blackwell home sheltered these eight people. Elizabeth was exhausted helping to serve meals to so many people. At teatime, she placed a bowl of honey on the table instead of sugar, explaining, "We've switched to using honey because sugar cane is grown by slaves."

The Coxes were amazed. "But Blackwell," Mr. Cox said, turning to Papa, "sugar is your business."

"That's true," Papa admitted. "For now it's all I know how to do to support my family. But I work against slavery as best I can. And using honey was my children's idea."

The visitors had not been long in the house before they commented on how worried all the Blackwells seemed about baby George. "Why, that child looks as healthy as any baby I've ever seen," Mrs. Cox said.

Elizabeth, not wanting to upset her mother, took Mrs. Cox aside to explain: "Four of Mama's babies died. We can't help being afraid George might die, too." To herself she thought, *it's like the cholera — no one knows why so many babies die or why people get cholera.* But George, fortunately, survived and grew.

Eliza Major was no longer their governess, for she had married Uncle Charles Lane, Mama's brother, who arrived in New York after many adventures in India. He and Eliza had known and liked each other in England. Together they opened their own school for young women; Marian and Elizabeth were among their pupils.

Elizabeth loved going to school. At least, she loved some subjects, especially music, French, and philosophy. One subject she did *not* love was anatomy, the study of the body. Just opening her book made her shudder. Who needed to know all that awful stuff about how the body worked?

One day, one of her teachers brought the eye of a bull into class. As she explained how the eye worked, Elizabeth tried to pay attention and learn. But just the sight of that revolting thing made her feel sicker every minute. It was like being seasick again. Also, she couldn't help picturing the bull itself with an empty eye socket, which made her feel much worse.

"Now, class, you will all file past my desk so you can look at the eye up close," said the teacher. Elizabeth tried to squint a bit as she passed the desk but she still got too good a look at the eye. It rested on a cushion of bloody fat and seemed to be staring straight at her. Sick to her stomach, and furious with herself for her weakness, she bolted from the classroom.

By this time, the Blackwells had moved to a house in Jersey City, on a hill overlooking the river that separated New Jersey from New York. From the porch, they could see the tall buildings of New York and could watch the boats on the river, including the ferryboat that took them to the city.

In December 1835, Elizabeth and Anna had just come out on the porch to go for a walk when the fire alarm rang out across the river. In the distance, they saw flames. "Papa, come quick, New York is burning!" Elizabeth cried. Papa ran out, took one look, dashed into the house for his coat, and ran for the ferry. "He has to protect the sugar refineries!" Elizabeth said. The whole family watched for three days as the fire raged, in agony because they had no way of knowing if Papa was safe. Elizabeth kept remem-

The Great Fire of 1835, New York City. (Corbis/Bettmann.)

bering the Bristol riots. Then, too, the family had watched and waited.

But now, as then, Papa came home safely. "The refineries were not touched," he said. "But from now on, I'll spend many nights in town to guard them." He told them that before the fire was controlled, some forty blocks of downtown New York and several hundred buildings were destroyed.

Life grew harder after the great fire because Papa's business began to fail. Mama struggled to feed the big family on less and less money, with her daughters helping.

Elizabeth, fourteen now, did her share of housework and sewing and child care, but always with a deep longing to find some work that would let her contribute to the wide world beyond her own home. In her diary she wrote: "How I do long for some end to act for, some end to be obtained in this life. ...to go on every day in much the same jog-trot manner without any object is very wearisome."

Once she did have the chance to help with a truly important project. Her twelve-year-old brother Sam brought home a runaway slave girl. She had been hiding out in the home of some Blackwell friends who believed her master had tracked her there. "We have to keep her hidden," Sam said. "If anyone finds her, they'll send her back into slavery!" Papa said that in a few weeks a ship would be leaving for England and that they would hide the girl until they could put her on board.

Elizabeth brought meals to the frightened girl, who hid in the attic so the neighbors would not see her through the windows. "You can wear these, I'm sure they'll fit you," she said, handing over warm clothes from her own cupboard. *I'm helping to fight slavery*, she thought excitedly during those weeks. *There has to be other real work I can find to do, too.*

In October 1836, when Elizabeth was fifteen, one of Papa's sugar refineries did burn down, as he feared. He had to close down his business. He did not seem healthy and he became so sad he even lost interest in the cause of abolition. Elizabeth poured her worries into her journal: "What Papa's

The Struggle to Free the Slaves

In the United States, the movement to free the slaves began about 1820 with the publication of anti-slavery articles in newspapers and magazines. In 1833, William Lloyd Garrison (a friend of Elizabeth's father) and a group of businessmen formed the American Anti-Slavery Society in Philadelphia. The term "abolitionist," meaning people who were against slavery, began to be used in about 1835. The abolitionists hid runaway slaves, helping them move from place to place until they reached Canada, where slavery was against the law. Many poems and novels were written to show the evils of slavery; many runaway slaves wrote about their own experiences.

plans for the future are we do not know.... I fear we shall not have much pleasure in life now."

Soon the family found out what Papa's plan was: they were to pack up once more and move to Cincinnati, Ohio. In the West, Papa was sure there were new business opportunities and a better life for his family. Elizabeth was happy. She didn't care where they lived; what mattered was that Papa seemed spirited and confident once again. She knew that many people in America looked to the West for a better future. Why not the Blackwells? Although Anna and Marian, old enough in their late teens to be considered adults, decided to stay in the East and take teaching jobs, the rest of the family would move. *Onward, westward!*

Cincinnati Harbor in the mid-1800s. (Cincinnati Historical Society.)

Why So Many Babies Died

At the beginning of the 1800s, studies in Europe indicated that about one-quarter of all children died before they reached the age of two. A major cause of death was malnutrition because mothers fed babies poor food (such as watery cereal or bread mixed with water) instead of breast milk. Many babies also died of such diseases as smallpox, diphtheria, pneumonia, cholera, and typhoid fever. As late as 1870, reliable records showed that about one-third of babies born in New York City died before their first birthday.

5

A TERRIBLE LOSS, STRUGGLING TO SURVIVE, AND A BRAVE NEW DIRECTION

"Is Papa going to die?" asked six-year-old George. Elizabeth, in a rush to get back to Papa's bedside, could only hug her little brother and answer, "We must keep praying that Papa will get better." She wished she had the courage to answer George honestly. It was summer and Papa had been sick since they arrived in Cincinnati in the spring. The doctors called it "bilious fever" and treated him with one medicine after another. But Elizabeth could tell they really didn't know what was wrong or what to do for him.

"Elizabeth, Papa has been asking for you!" Mama called. Elizabeth sank down on her knees next to Papa's bed. She held his hand. She knew he was leaving them. Her heart could not bear the pain. "I love you, Papa."

The room filled with all the family members who had moved West. Two of Papa's friends, and the doctor who had not been able to help him, were also there. Even so, Elizabeth, holding her father's hand until the end, felt completely alone with her sorrow.

The family waited until the day after the funeral to face their problems. They were living in a strange city, a place so new they had scarcely unpacked. Their debts were much bigger than the small amount of money Papa had left them. Elizabeth, only seventeen, felt as if she had been grown-up for years. She and Mama and Sam, fourteen, and Henry, thirteen, needed to decide together how to earn a living for themselves and the four younger children – Emily, Ellen, Howard, and George.

Elizabeth had an idea. She was not sure it was a good one. But she knew it was the only thing they could try. So she announced: "We will start a boarding school."

"There are already a lot of schools in this town," Henry objected.

"Then there must be room for one more," Elizabeth said with more confidence than she felt. "I will teach and maybe Anna and Marian will come to Cincinnati and teach, too."

"Before we worry about who will teach," Mama said gently, "we had better find some pupils."

So Elizabeth wrote booklets describing their school and Mama, who had never before in her life been active outside her own home, went bravely from door to door handing out the booklets.

Only a few days later, Elizabeth found herself teaching four paying pupils plus her own four younger sisters and brothers. Before long, Anna and Marian arrived from the East and started teaching as well. Samuel found work as a bookkeeper and Henry as an errand boy in a shop. Their wages were necessary, since so few pupils were paying to attend the little school.

Elizabeth did not like teaching. Years later, she wrote in her journal that she was afraid of her pupils because she did not know enough about how to make them behave or how to teach them. But Papa had taught her the importance of education and she tried to do the best she could.

After a few years of struggle, with fewer and fewer paying students, the Blackwells gave up the school. The family could manage without it, because Henry and Sam had good jobs. But what would Elizabeth do next? She still longed to do something hard and important but the only work she had ever done was to teach. So when she was offered a chance to start a small school for girls in Henderson, Kentucky, she said to Anna, "At least it will be an adventure for us to teach in strange places." Anna was going to teach music in Columbus, Ohio, while Marian stayed home to help Mama with the children.

"But Kentucky!" Anna protested. "It is slave country, you know."

"Then I will find out for myself what slavery is like."

Elizabeth was twenty-three when she set out on her new life in Kentucky. She arrived on a Saturday. "I will begin teaching on Monday," she told Dr. Wilson, who had hired her.

Dr. Wilson laughed. "Miss Blackwell, you must be one of those Northerners who does everything in a hurry! We need time to fix up the schoolhouse, to paint it, to tell the students we'll be opening sometime soon – "

"Monday." Elizabeth's voice was firm.

Elizabeth herself supervised the men who hammered and scrubbed and painted all weekend. On Monday morning, fourteen young girls were seated in school facing their new teacher.

Elizabeth tried to make her students care about learning. "Education will open the world to you," she told them. But she heard them talking among themselves, saying that marriage was what they wanted, not education.

Elizabeth wrote home that she laughed when the people in Henderson were surprised her teeth were so white. "This is tobacco country and everyone in town seems to use it," she wrote. The tobacco turned their teeth yellow.

Away from her family, Elizabeth was so lonely that she was grateful for any invitation to a local home. So when she was asked to tea one afternoon, she put on her best dress. Her hostess greeted her in a comfortable parlor where a silver tea tray was set with pretty china. It was a chilly day and Elizabeth, invited to sit down and make herself at home, chose a chair near the fireplace. After a few minutes, though, she began to feel hot, and she leaned toward the side of her chair that was farther away from the fire.

"Miss Blackwell, I can see you find the fire too warm," her hostess said. Setting down her teacup, the woman clapped her hands together. "Lily, come here, quickly, girl! Come and stand in front of the fire."

Before Elizabeth could protest, Lily, a small black child, was standing between her and the fire. *The heat must be unbearable*, Elizabeth thought in horror. *How could anyone use a child as if she were a wooden screen, an object, as if she had no feelings at all! I hate slavery*, she thought. *I can't stand to have that poor child suffer for my sake.*

"I must leave," she said, suddenly standing up. She bit her tongue to keep from adding a polite excuse. Her hostess did not deserve one.

Elizabeth knew there was no point voicing her objections to slavery. But neither could she go on living where it was practiced. At the end of the term, she left Kentucky and went home to Cincinnati.

And now that I'm home, what will I do? When will I discover my life's goal?

Slave auction in the South. (Culver Pictures.)

Though many of the young women she knew had marriage as their goal, Elizabeth was searching for something more. Yet she did fall in love that autumn and being in love made her happy. *Wouldn't it be possible to combine marriage with some other important life work?* she wondered. The young man was well educated and interesting— so interesting that Elizabeth excitedly shared with him her interests in philosophy and politics, in how society might be changed for the better. "Miss Blackwell, such ideas for a woman!" he said. "You should not be worrying about such things. Let men solve the problems. Read poetry, if you have to read books."

I don't HAVE to read books, I want to! I want to think and plan and be useful. How foolish I was to think he would want a wife like that. Greatly disappointed, Elizabeth let him know she was no longer interested in him.

When her mother suggested that Elizabeth visit Mrs. Donaldson, a friend of Mama's who was dying of cancer, Elizabeth's first thought was, *I don't like to be around sick people.* Then she felt ashamed. She had always liked Mary Donaldson and her illness was a tragedy.

She went to see Mrs. Donaldson the next day. Within a few minutes she felt trapped. The room was too warm, too dark, and smelled of sickness. Elizabeth wanted to run back outside into the air and the sunlight. But poor Mrs. Donaldson would never run out into the sunlight again. Elizabeth forced herself to sit still.

"Your mother sent you to visit me, I know," Mary Donaldson said in her weak voice. "But still, it was kind of you to come."

Elizabeth tried not to fidget.

"Tell me what you have been doing, Elizabeth."

"Oh, trying to teach girls who don't want to learn!" She sighed. "Teaching is just not the right work for me. I want — I want to do something that's so hard it uses all of me." *Why am I bothering poor Mary Donaldson with my problems?* she wondered.

"You should become a doctor," Mrs. Donaldson said and her voice was suddenly stronger, as if she was putting all her energy into this idea.

"A doctor! Women aren't doctors."

"Well, they *should* be. I've had so much time to think while I lie here helpless and I've thought and thought that there should be women doctors. Women are too modest to be examined by men doctors. If I only had a woman doctor to treat me — she would spare me so much embarrassment, so much misery!" Mrs. Donaldson leaned closer to Elizabeth, who could see that every movement gave her pain. "You could do it, Elizabeth. You are strong and intelligent. You could be the first and other women would follow. Then your life would have the meaning you are looking for."

Elizabeth thought of the day her teacher ordered her to look closely at the bull's eye. How sickening the thing had been! In her mind she saw again the cloudy eye that still seemed to be staring. Shuddering, she recalled how she'd run from the room. Wouldn't learning to be a doctor mean looking at many upsetting things?

She didn't want to tell Mrs. Donaldson any of this. And she would never hurt her feelings by admitting she didn't like to be with sick people. So she said, "But when there haven't been any women doctors, it would be so hard – "

Then she realized what she'd just said. *It would be so hard.* For a woman to become a doctor — could anything be more difficult? And wasn't that what she always wanted, to prove she could do something truly hard?

Women Doctors in Earlier Centuries

Women had practiced medicine in some parts of the world many years before Elizabeth's time. In ancient Egypt during the reign of Queen Hatshepsut, women attended medical schools. Histories of early Greek and Roman times mention women as medical students and doctors. A woman named *Aspasia,* who specialized in women's diseases and in childbirth, was quoted in Greek and Latin medical books for more than a thousand years. Laws written in Europe between the seventh and ninth centuries mention women doctors. In the eleventh century, *Trotula* and other women taught medicine at the first European medical school, at Salerno in what is now Italy. In the eighteenth century, *Anna Morandi Manzolini* was professor of anatomy at the University of Bologna, also in Italy. And a Scotswoman actually named *Elizabeth Blackwell* studied medicine in the eighteenth century and published an important book on the use of herbs in medicine.

6

DOING THE IMPOSSIBLE, IMPRACTICAL, AND UNWOMANLY

"I'm thinking of trying to become a doctor," Elizabeth said hesitantly to her good friend Harriet Beecher Stowe, the writer. "What do you think?"

"I will ask my husband for his opinion," Harriet answered.

Elizabeth was surprised. She had expected Harriet to reply right away that of course a woman could do anything. Harriet certainly lived her own life that way. She was the wife of a busy professor and had a large family. Still, in spite of all the work of running her household, in spite of endless noise and interruptions, she was always writing: stories, novels, essays.

A few days later, Elizabeth returned to the Stowe home. The two women sat in Harriet's parlor, with Harriet's two-year-old daughter on her mother's knee and her two little sons playing noisily at the other end of the room. Yet a pile of paper with a story Harriet was writing lay on the table next to her chair and Elizabeth noticed that her friend's fingers were ink-stained. Harriet was a dedicated mother but she was a dedicated writer, too.

Harriet Beecher Stowe

The writer was born in Connecticut in 1811. Her father, Lyman Beecher, was a minister; her brother, Henry Ward Beecher, was a minister and writer; and her sister, Catherine E. Beecher, wrote books on how to turn a house into a comfortable home. In 1832, the family moved to Cincinnati, near the Blackwells, and in 1836 Harriet married Calvin Ellis Stowe, a professor of religion. When her sixth child died of cholera in 1849, Harriet felt she understood how painful it was for slave mothers to be separated from their children and vowed to do something to help the slaves. What she did was write *Uncle Tom's Cabin*, a novel about runaway slaves published in 1852, which caused a sensation. One of the most popular books ever published, *Uncle Tom's Cabin* was considered one of the factors that helped start the Civil War.

UNCLE TOM'S CABIN;

OR,

LIFE AMONG THE LOWLY.

BY

HARRIET BEECHER STOWE.

VOL. I.

BOSTON:
JOHN P. JEWETT & COMPANY.
CLEVELAND, OHIO:
JEWETT, PROCTOR & WORTHINGTON.
1852.

FIRST EDITION, IN THE EXCESSIVELY RARE
RED CLOTH PRESENTATION BINDING

Title page from the first edition of Uncle Tom's
Cabin. *(Corbis / Bettmann.)*

"It would indeed be wonderful for women, for mothers, if there could be women doctors," Harriet said. Elizabeth nodded. So far Harriet sounded very much like Mary Donaldson. "But my husband and I have talked it over," Harriet went on. "You could never be a doctor, Elizabeth! It is an impossible notion. You would only destroy yourself trying."

Elizabeth was very disappointed but she did not argue. She simply said, "I will not destroy myself." And she thought, *but I will become a doctor.* She looked with affection at the small child on Harriet's lap. Now and then,

No Rights For Married Women

There were some excellent reasons why Elizabeth and her sisters were not eager to marry. Married women at this time could not own property, had no legal rights to their own earnings, or (in case of divorce) even their own children. They were essentially the property of their husbands. If Elizabeth had been married, she would almost certainly not have worked as a teacher, since it was considered improper for married women to work, but if she had, her salary would have belonged to her husband. She would not be able to move from place to place for her medical studies without her husband's permission. And no woman, married or single, could vote or sign legal papers.

when she thought she was in love, she had wondered if she would marry and have children. But now, with a difficult goal to work toward, Elizabeth thought it might be best to stay single. A single woman could live where she liked and do as she chose. Her time and money were her own.

Elizabeth said good-bye to Harriet and her children and walked home making plans in her head. Money! She would need money for school. How was she to get it? She could teach, but while she was teaching she would not be moving closer to becoming a doctor. *Well, Elizabeth,* she said to herself, *you wanted life to be hard! Is this hard enough?*

Back home, Elizabeth wrote letters to a few doctors who were friends of her family, asking their advice. Their answers were a lot like Harriet's. As Elizabeth wrote in her journal, they all thought her goal was "a good idea but impossible to accomplish." But she also wrote that when people told her she could not do what she wanted, she did not feel like giving up. Instead she felt encouraged to try hard to do it. And she wrote, "My own family showed the warmest sympathy with my plan."

Soon the plan required her to move away from her family. Through a friend, Elizabeth was offered a job teaching music in a small school in Asheville, North Carolina run by the Reverend John Dickson. But this minister had once been a doctor, had a library full of medical books, and promised to teach her chemistry, physics, and even some anatomy!

During the day, Elizabeth taught piano, and sometimes reading, to girls. By the end of the day she was worn out, but turning to medical studies in the evening gave her a new burst of energy. "It is quite amazing how fast you learn, Miss Blackwell," the Reverend Dr. Dickson said. "I myself never liked the study of medicine but you seem to be born for it."

To Elizabeth, who felt a new world opening to her each evening, it was amazing that anyone could not like studying medicine.

She was enjoying life altogether. "My brain is as busy as can be and consequently I am happy," she wrote Mama, "for one is only miserable when...lazy, wasting time and doing no good to self or anybody else."

But some of the teachers in the school seemed to resent her joy. One day, another woman teacher brought in a dead

Nineteenth Century Beliefs About Women

Women and men were seen as totally different beings, with almost nothing in common between the two sexes. Qualities such as bravery, daring, and strength were qualities of men. Women were believed to be passive by nature. Strong or brave women were considered "unnatural." A popular magazine of the time, *Godey's Lady's Book*, called a true woman "delicate and timid"; she "required protection" and "possessed a sweet dependency."

beetle, wrapped in her handkerchief. "I know you will enjoy having a body to dissect, Miss Blackwell," she taunted, expecting Elizabeth to back away in horror.

Elizabeth hid her disgust, placed the insect in a seashell, and held it down with a hairpin. She did not want to be laughed at, but it was hard to force herself to actually cut into the beetle.

Finally, she gripped her knife and cut off the head. "Notice how it has no brains," she announced to the watching teachers, hoping to sound like a cool scientist but hearing how shaky her voice was. Then she jabbed into the beetle's body with the knife. She found nothing awful inside, only some yellow dust. *I'll never be timid about dissecting again*, she thought.

And indeed when Dr. Dickson said one evening, "Here is a real human skeleton I borrowed for you to study," she found the skeleton more interesting than upsetting.

Elizabeth did not work all the time. When she was invited to parties she accepted gladly. She often played the piano and even did magic tricks at these events.

On Sunday, she taught four little slave girls, aged eight to twelve, at a Sunday school. It was illegal to teach slaves in any other kind of school. She felt it was wrong that the only thing slaves were allowed to learn was religion, when religion should have taught that slavery was wrong.

When the Reverend Dr. Dickson closed his school for lack of students, Elizabeth moved to Charleston, South Carolina, to stay with the family of his brother, Dr. Samuel Dickson, a well-known physician. This Dr.

Dickson found Elizabeth a job teaching music at a boarding school.

Once more Elizabeth taught in the daytime, saving her salary for medical school, and studied medicine at night. She needed all her courage and determination the evening Dr. Dickson said, "If you ever intend to be a surgeon, Elizabeth, you must study books on surgery."

She took the big books he handed her, but it was a long time before she could make herself open them. They were full of realistic scenes of knives and blood, and described people's pain all too clearly. Elizabeth's dreams became nightmares. But she wanted to be a surgeon and she made herself study the surgery books carefully.

Everyone she asked told Elizabeth that Philadelphia, Pennsylvania was the center for medicine in the United States. So in May 1847 she moved there, hoping to be admitted to one of the city's four major medical schools. Meanwhile, she studied in a private school of anatomy run by a Dr. Allen. Once he was convinced of her determination and willingness to work, the doctor was kind to his unusual student. He never made her feel she could not learn medicine because she was a woman. Elizabeth never told him the smell in his dissecting rooms made her so sick that she could hardly eat even when she was back in her boarding house!

At her first lesson, Dr. Allen brought out a preserved human arm, yellow from soaking in a bucket of evil-smelling disinfectant. "We will begin to learn the structure of the wrist," he said, beginning to dissect.

Elizabeth fought to keep from giving in to her dizziness. This was a harder test than the one with the dead bug. She forced herself to watch closely as Dr. Allen inserted a knife into the wrist. But this time she was fascinated by what she saw as Dr. Allen dissected it, exposing tendons, nerves, and muscles. She wrote in her journal: "The beauty of the tendons and exquisite arrangement of this part of the body struck my artistic sense."

After that evening, Elizabeth herself worked at dissecting the wrist, spending long hours among Dr. Allen's men students in the smelly room.

She learned a great deal with Dr. Allen, but his school could not give her a degree that would allow her to practice medicine. It was time to apply to medical school.

Elizabeth visited the professors at all the medical schools in Philadelphia. Some laughed at her, some were coldly polite, and some offered sympathy but the final results were the same. No, a woman could not be admitted to their medical school. Dr. Warrington, a friendly doctor who let her come to his private classes and even allowed her to visit patients with him, said: "Your only hope, Elizabeth, is to go to Paris and wear men's clothes — there you can attend medical school as a man."

"I will not! That will not help other women become doctors!"

She wrote application after application, twenty-nine in all. As the weeks passed, the rejection letters poured in, twenty-eight of them by the time the fall term began. In those twenty-eight medical schools, young men were preparing to become doctors, but not a single woman studied with them.

Elizabeth went to New York to visit her sister Anna, who was earning her living writing for newspapers. She returned to Philadelphia feeling dejected. If only she could have the kind of success at becoming a doctor that Anna was having as a journalist! Looking over her mail, she saw the letter from Geneva College, the twenty-ninth medical school. The last rejection, she thought, as she opened it. But it wasn't a rejection! Dr. Charles Lee, the Dean, wrote that the students had voted to accept her and that therefore they and the professors would welcome her.

Elizabeth shouted for joy. "I'm leaving for medical school!"

A LADY MEDICAL STUDENT IS EITHER MAD OR BAD

"Leaving Philadelphia on November 4, I hastened through New York, traveled all night, and reached... Geneva at eleven p.m. on November 6," wrote Elizabeth in her journal. Her problems began the next day.

"But the sign in your window says Room For Rent," Elizabeth pointed out to the landlady who was trying to shut the door in her face.

The woman muttered something about "no lady" and "medicine" and slammed the door.

Elizabeth was amazed that strangers in the small town of Geneva already knew why she had come to their town. Not only knew but objected!

At the next boarding house, the landlady at least gave Elizabeth a fuller explanation before turning her away: "I'd be out of business in a hurry if I rented a room to a woman wanting to be a doctor. Why, all my respectable boarders would move out!"

Walking the streets of Geneva in the cold November rain, Elizabeth thought, *how can I be a student without a room to sleep and study in?*

The next landlady, a Mrs. Waller, made it just as plain that Elizabeth was not welcome. But this time Elizabeth insisted on being admitted and sitting down before making her point with great firmness. Mrs. Waller looked like an intelligent woman. "You would not let other people make up your mind for you, Mrs. Waller. I am not a monster, I'm only a lady who needs a home."

Mrs. Waller shook her head. "My other guests would be rude to you, Miss Blackwell. You would not be happy here."

"Never mind happiness. I only ask for shelter," Elizabeth said. "Will you show me where to put my bags?"

Mrs. Waller smiled and gave in. The bedroom was small and dark, at the top of many stairs, and heated only by a tiny stove. But the little room was warm and welcoming compared to the people in the dining room. Voices stopped when Elizabeth entered. Women scowled and turned their faces away. No one replied to Elizabeth's "Good evening." She ate her dinner in lonely silence and climbed back up to her room. Elizabeth, twenty-six now, had grown up a much loved daughter in a lively home; Geneva was certainly a new experience.

Life at the college was strange and confusing. Facing her first day's classes had been hard but the next few days were even worse. The noisy halls were crowded with young men who knew where their next class was and who had books and equipment and friends. None of this was true for Elizabeth. Where was she supposed to go? How would she get books? Who would tell her how to make up the lessons she'd missed during the five weeks before she'd arrived?

The first truly friendly person she met was the anatomy professor, Dr. Webster. He told Elizabeth: "We have been needing a lady student!"

Eventually, Elizabeth learned her way around and caught up on missed lessons. But life outside school continued to be a strain. In the street, little boys gawked at her, pointing and laughing. Adults first stared, then turned away rudely as they passed. She often stayed at the college until after midnight, working in the dissecting rooms, partly to learn as much as possible but also because it was a relief to walk home when the streets were empty. She only learned much later that the citizens of Geneva thought any woman who wanted to be a doctor was either crazy or evil, "mad or bad."

Fortunately, the other students treated her well. Still, Elizabeth knew she had to be careful not to be too friendly to these young men. She wanted to be regarded only as a fellow student, not as a woman looking for romance. Once, a folded piece of paper, very likely a rude note, sailed across the classroom and landed on Elizabeth's sleeve. She ignored it and continued writing until the end of class when she brushed it to the floor without looking up. She wasn't tested this way again.

One day Dr. Webster told her, "Miss Blackwell, I think you will want to stay away from class for this next subject."

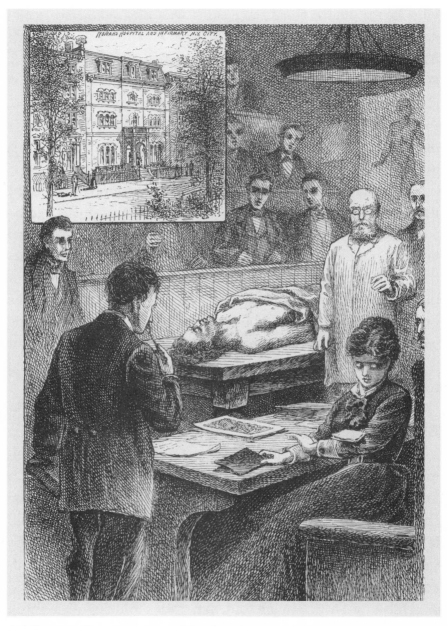

A fellow student tries to get Elizabeth's attention. (Corbis/Bettmann.)

He was about to discuss sex and reproduction and thought Elizabeth, the other students, and even he himself would be uncomfortable if she were present.

Elizabeth sent him a letter. Everything about the human body is holy, she wrote. Besides, she and all the other students were preparing to help women bear children. How could anything about this subject be improper?

Dr. Webster gave in. He read Elizabeth's letter to the class and then invited Elizabeth into the lecture room. For once, Dr. Webster taught the subject seriously, without a lot of rude jokes. And the students listened without hooting, whistling, and stamping their feet. The lectures had never been as successful as they were with Elizabeth present.

But she paid a price. She told her sister Anna long afterward: "I ate very little, hoping this would keep me from changing color when the subject matter was embarrassing." Starving probably didn't prevent blushing but Elizabeth certainly tried her best!

She also paid a high price for her decision not to socialize with the other students. She was very lonely and she expected to go on being lonely. In December, her second month of medical school, she wrote in her journal, "I must work by myself all life long."

Christmas came and her fellow students went home for the holiday but she could not afford the time or the money to travel all the way to Cincinnati. In her little room in Mrs. Waller's house, she ate her Christmas treat: twenty-five cents worth of raisins and almonds. And she read the "Christmas Annual," a little magazine the Blackwell brothers and sisters wrote each year and sent to all family members. Elizabeth had written some of the stories in it.

But even on Christmas, Elizabeth had work to do. She spent the day writing letters to hospitals, hoping to find one where she could work between her first and second years of medical school. So far, all of her medical education had been "book learning," plus dissection. She thought, *I want to work with real patients. Surely if I can get into medical school, I can find a hospital to work at.*

First, the rejections poured in, as they had from medical schools. But just as Geneva College had finally accepted Elizabeth, a hospital accepted her at last: the women's hospital at Blockley Almshouse in Philadelphia.

Nineteenth Century Medical Training

Medical students were not required to have a college degree or any special formal schooling before entering medical school. They only had to study for three years with a doctor, and then attend two years of medical school. Each of these "years" only lasted four months, from October through January. During the second year, the courses simply repeated the first year's material. This gave students a chance to learn whatever they hadn't learned the first time around but did not teach them anything new.

8

HELPING TO HEAL AT THE WOMEN'S HOSPITAL

Elizabeth, looking up from her unpacking, met the curious stares of two women patients who peeked at her from around the edge of the slightly open door to her new room. The women giggled and ran away. Elizabeth got up and opened the door wider. *They're only curious about me, so let them get a good look*, she thought and went back to putting her books on a shelf and hanging up her few dresses. Now and then she looked up and saw more patients who found a reason to wander by and stare in at the new "doctor." Elizabeth smiled at them. A few smiled back and a few made faces at her, but most just looked embarrassed. When she finished unpacking, Elizabeth moved her desk opposite the keyhole so that the patients could watch her even with the door closed and satisfy their curiosity.

An almshouse was a home for poor people who had no other place to go. About 2,000 people lived at Blockley. So many of them were sick that the women's hospital was always extremely crowded.

Elizabeth's room was located in a part of the hospital where the women patients were very sick, some with contagious diseases which patients could catch from each other, some with mental problems which caused strange or even wild behavior.

Elizabeth was grateful to be working with patients. But she didn't know exactly what she was supposed to do. She wasn't a fully trained doctor but she didn't fit in with the nurses either.

While learning medicine was Elizabeth's goal, she was also determined to help the sick women. She was shocked by the stories they told. Many were servants who had been

Blockley Almshouse, Philadelphia. (Culver Pictures.)

badly treated by their employers. Others were unmarried women with babies and no way to earn a living. Elizabeth offered them sympathy and comfort, while also asking questions about their symptoms and noting the treatments prescribed by the doctors.

Some of the treatments common at the time were horrifying. "Think you can be a doctor, do you?" taunted one of the young doctors who resented Elizabeth's presence. "Can you stand to watch while I bleed this patient?" He applied leeches to the skin of a young woman. The leeches were soon fat with the poor patient's blood. "You don't have any idea why we do that, do you?" the doctor asked rudely.

Elizabeth answered: "Certainly I know. Bleeding patients helps to rid them of inflammations." She had been taught this fact (now long since found to be false) in medical school but until today she had never seen blood removed from already weak, sick patients in order to make them well!

But some people at Blockley were helpful to Elizabeth. One was Dr. Nathan D. Benedict, the head doctor, who was kind to everyone and gentle with every patient. "Every woman has been important to someone," he said. The other was the hospital matron, or head nurse, a changeable woman who was sometimes quiet and ladylike but at other times screamed out punishments to disorderly patients (showers, which the women hated, were her favorite punishment). She ran the hospital by sitting in her large room, feet on a velvet footstool, and giving orders.

With these two important people on her side, Elizabeth wrote, she "had free entry to all the women's wards, and was soon on good terms with the nurses." But not all the patients accepted her. "Ain't no woman going to treat me, you don't tell me you're a doctor!" shouted one sick old woman in pain. How could Elizabeth possibly be a doctor when no lady was?

The young doctors, just as much against the notion of a woman in medicine as the angry old woman was, showed their resentment in their own way. They all marched out of a ward when Elizabeth entered it. And, although it was the custom to write the facts about each patient's condition and treatment on the chart attached to her bed, the doctors stopped writing on the charts when Elizabeth was around. She was left to guess what might be wrong with a sick

The Scourge of Typhus

Transmitted to people by the body louse, an insect which lives on unwashed bodies and dirty clothing, typhus causes fever, headache, chills, aches, and a rash. The worst epidemics occur during wars and famines when living conditions are bad. The death rate has ranged between 10 and 40 percent in different epidemics. Today typhus is treated effectively with antibiotics. Elizabeth, once she became a doctor, was wiser than most other medical people of her time in stressing that, to maintain good health, people should keep themselves and their surroundings clean.

woman and what the doctors were doing to treat her. "They want to make my work harder," she muttered, staring at a blank chart. "All right, I'll work harder. But I'll manage. They can't stop me."

But a time came when the young men doctors no longer wanted to keep Elizabeth from treating patients, when the hospital was so overflowing with desperately sick patients that even a woman doctor was welcome. "Blackwell, we need you here!" was the cry Elizabeth often heard now. A typhus epidemic had broken out among newly arrived immigrants from Ireland. Some had become sick on the ship that brought them (and the disease was sometimes known as "ship fever"). Some became ill after landing. Because there weren't enough beds, women had to lie on the hospital floors. Elizabeth and the doctors and nurses, hurrying through the wards, had to be careful not to step on patients, some nearly hidden under sheets. Sometimes women died as they lay on the floor.

Elizabeth tended patients night and day. But even as she offered treatment and comfort, her mind was storing up details of typhus infection: its symptoms, how it developed, which treatments helped or failed to help. She had decided to write her medical school graduation thesis, a long essay, on this disease.

To learn even more, she attended autopsies (detailed examinations of the bodies of dead patients) of typhus victims. She took notes on the condition of organs such as the brain, lungs, and liver. Everything she learned, from patients, from autopsies, from books, plus her own ideas on disease and on health would go into her thesis, to be handed in during her second year of medical school.

Elizabeth was not afraid of catching typhus or any other disease she encountered at Blockley. She believed that cleanliness and plenty of fresh air and exercise kept her safe. But her mother, back home in Cincinnati, wrote her long worried letters. Mama's main question was: why did Elizabeth choose to live this strange, dangerous life? Though proud of Elizabeth, Mama would have been happier if her daughter had simply married and lived as other women's daughters did.

When she was not trying to help the women patients in the hospital, Elizabeth cared for their babies, who were often sick too. One day she treated a baby who was suffering from ophthalmia, a serious eye infection. But even as she did what she could for the child, she knew that medical science did not really have any successful method of treating this disease. *Poor little girl*, thought Elizabeth, *what will happen to her if her eyesight is destroyed?* Because she wanted to be a surgeon, Elizabeth was unusually conscious of the importance of good eyesight.

By September 22, her last day at Blockley, Elizabeth had finished writing her thesis on typhus and given a copy to the kind Dr. Benedict. It was time to move on, to return to school for her second and last year of formal medical training. How did she feel on that evening, after the insults, the challenges, the education that had all been part of her experience at the great hospital? Elizabeth wrote: "How glad I am, tomorrow, tomorrow, I go home to my friends! And yet...I almost regretted that I was going to leave."

9

FIRST WOMAN DOCTOR— AT LAST!

"Hurray! Look! It's Blackwell - Blackwell's come back!" The shouts echoed through the halls of Geneva Medical College. Elizabeth knew that if she were male, the other returning students would be clapping her on the back. But she was a lady and they were trying to be gentlemen, so they were shouting with joy, smiling widely, and shaking her hand.

Elizabeth was happy that her fellow students welcomed her back with such enthusiasm. How different this year was from last year! Elizabeth knew her way around the college well; the other second-year students knew and liked her. Her landlady, Mrs. Waller, actually treated her like an old friend as she helped Elizabeth carry her belongings upstairs to her little room.

She could even feel a difference in the streets of Geneva. She was no longer treated as if she were some strange life form. It's true that she was mainly ignored, but to have her presence taken for granted was a great improvement over being deliberately snubbed, even taunted.

She wrote, "I settled down for winter work. Bright visions of usefulness have been floating around me." First she met with Dr. Webster, the anatomy professor, who was her advisor. She waited anxiously as he read her thesis on typhus. "Excellent, Miss Blackwell, most impressive work! I intend to read your paper to my first class of the year." This he did, with obvious pride, and at the end the class applauded.

Elizabeth also discussed her future with Dr. Webster, for it would not be long before she had all the medical training Geneva College had to offer. After helping him during an operation, Elizabeth said warily, "I want to be a surgeon." She braced herself to be told that women could never be surgeons.

But Dr. Webster surprised her. "A fine ambition. I know you will be a successful surgeon, Miss Blackwell."

In November, Elizabeth had a welcome visit from her seventeen-year-old brother Howard. Elizabeth had not seen him for three years and the change in him amazed her. "I have decided to go to England to help our English relatives manage their iron foundry," he announced.

His big sister said admiringly, "They will be lucky to have you. You have become a man, Howie."

Howard wasn't the only Blackwell preparing to sail across the Atlantic. Anna was moving to Paris. "She writes that she's been hired to translate French books into English," Elizabeth told Howie. And she added, "My dream is to go to Paris, too."

"What would you do there?" Howie asked.

"I'd seek advanced training in medicine," Elizabeth said. "There is so much more to learn."

About Howard's visit she wrote in her journal: "How good...to see a brother!...I did more laughing than I've done for months. His visit did me real good, for I have been so lonely."

Elizabeth's second Christmas in Geneva was much less lonely, and far merrier, than her first. Her English cousin, Kenyon Blackwell, arrived for a visit and brought her scientific books from England. Together they took long walks and read the Blackwell family "Christmas Annual." They laughed at the pen and ink drawings of little stick figures that illustrated the pages.

But Elizabeth spent New Year's Eve alone. Perhaps her experience of often being alone made her sympathetic to those who had no one else to turn to. For example, on January 11 she wrote, "I called to see a pretty blind girl operated on this morning.... Poor child! She has no protector.... Such are the women I long to surround with my stronger arm."

Final exams took place in January. "No need for you to worry," her fellow students told her. They were right. But some of the college officials considered refusing to give her a degree because she was a woman.

Dr. Webster angrily defended her. "Miss Blackwell has passed every course with honors!" Soon, all the grades were in and he was able to add: "Miss Blackwell has finished *first* in her class." She would certainly be granted her degree.

A Comment
On Elizabeth's Graduation

The *Boston Medical Journal* complained that
Elizabeth "had been...led to aspire to honors and
duties which, by the order of nature and common
consent of the world, devolve alone upon men."

Graduation was to take place on January 23, 1849 in the
Presbyterian church. Another brother, Henry, would travel
to Geneva to be with Elizabeth and represent the Blackwell
family.

Elizabeth had not bought any new clothes for years. But
feeling she owed it to the college to be well dressed on graduation day, she purchased an elegant black silk dress with
white lace at the cuffs and neckline. With it she wore a cape
trimmed in black silk fringe.

Elizabeth refused to march in the procession of graduates because, she said, to do so would not be ladylike. And
the ceremony was exciting enough for her without that. She
described the day in glowing terms: "'twas bright and beautiful and very gratifying. Great curiosity was felt....All the
ladies collected in the entry and let me pass between their
ranks and several spoke to me most kindly." The church
was so filled with the women of Geneva and surrounding
towns, curious to see a woman actually become a Doctor of

Medicine, that there was almost no room for the graduating students.

Dr. Charles Lee, the college Dean, who had escorted Elizabeth to her first class, gave the graduation speech. His principal topic: Elizabeth Blackwell and the successful experiment of admitting a woman to medical school. When Elizabeth was handed her diploma she vowed that she would try all her life "to shed honor on this diploma."

Later that day, wrote Elizabeth, "my room was thronged with visitors…but my past experience had given me a useful and permanent lesson at the outset of life as to the very shallow nature of popularity."

➤ By 1910, the year of Elizabeth's death, there were 7,399 women doctors in the United States. By 1985, the number increased to 80,725.

➤ Today, women make up about 18 percent of all physicians in the United States and about 46 percent of medical students.

➤ Elizabeth's early ambition to become a surgeon was revolutionary, but in 1994, according to the Association of Women Surgeons, there were more than 17,000 women surgeons in the United States.

➤ In 1988, Dr. Gertrude Elion became the latest of several women to be awarded the Nobel Prize in Medicine.

Elizabeth Blackwell, Doctor of Medicine at last, 1848. (Courtesy, NYU Downtown Hospital.)

It was Dr. Elizabeth Blackwell who woke up on the morning of January 24, 1849, ready to begin her life as a physician.

10

DISASTER STRIKES IN PARIS

Elizabeth Blackwell, M.D. paid a visit to the University of Pennsylvania, which had, of course, refused to admit her when she applied. Now they were happy to welcome her — but only for a short visit. She attended some lectures but was not admitted for further training. She did not expect other American schools to treat her any better. "Paris is the place to try," she wrote her family.

Before leaving for Europe, Elizabeth went to visit her mother, sisters, and brothers in Cincinnati. She had not been home for almost five years. Henry and Samuel had just become partners in a hardware business. Ellen was an artist, whose paintings decorated the walls of the Blackwell home.

Elizabeth's talk with her younger sister Emily produced some surprising news. "I am determined to become a doctor," Emily said.

Immediately, a dream began to take form for Elizabeth. "I see us practicing medicine together someday," she said. "We'll share an office, share the patients. But, you know, it's a hard road for a woman."

Emily said, "Do you think I haven't noticed what your life has been like? I'm willing to struggle, too."

Mama made it clear that, proud as she was of her daughters, she still wished one of them would marry. Elizabeth said, "I believe in marriage and I hope to marry one day." Now that she had reached one major goal, she could begin to think of others.

Before going to Paris, Elizabeth stopped in England to see her cousin Kenyon in Birmingham, England. Then she traveled on to Paris. Disappointment followed at once. The hospitals would not admit her for work or study. She was not considered a doctor, merely a woman who did not know her proper place. Finally, one doctor made a suggestion Elizabeth liked. "You should enter La Maternité," he said. "It is a hospital where women go to have their babies. There you would gain more experience delivering babies and caring for women and infants than you could gain anywhere else."

But La Maternité would not admit Elizabeth as a doctor, only as a trainee to become a midwife, a kind of special nurse who helps women through childbirth. Elizabeth explained to Anna that she would have to live at La Maternité during her training. Life there would involve "…a strict imprisonment, very poor lodging and food, some rather menial services, and the loss of three or four nights' sleep every week."

Anna was shocked. "But you are a doctor! Why should you be treated that way?"

"I won't mind, because I will learn so much. And when I leave there, I'll find a place to study surgery."

When Elizabeth entered La Maternité on June 30, 1849, she was immediately asked if she would like to spend her first night in the room where the babies were born. In her journal, she described the experience: "...beds all around, a fire on the hearth, ...and in the center a large wooden stand with sides, on which the little new-comers, lightly swathed and ticketed, are ranged side by side." Eight babies were born that night, a record. Each was "swathed" or wrapped up in a tiny jacket and a blanket, then "ticketed" or labeled with its mother's last name and whether it was a boy or a girl. The babies seemed to like company, for Elizabeth noted, "...there was very little crying all the time they lay there together."

But for Elizabeth, who valued privacy, the hardest part of her new life was living in one dormitory room with fifteen other young women. The students even took baths in groups, in a room with six tubs. Bathtime was lively, with students splashing each other and talking and singing together, but Elizabeth would have preferred a quiet, solitary bath.

The Voluntary Prisoner, as Elizabeth called herself, managed to arrange a sort of study area by placing a chair and books behind her bed and hanging her clothes in front of the bed as a kind of curtain. But there was no hiding from the noise! The other girls were less serious than

Elizabeth. For fun they rolled their iron beds around the room, slamming them into each other with a great clanging noise.

There was never enough sleep or food, always too much work. Worn out from caring for patients all night, Elizabeth would sweep floors and attend lectures in the daytime. But she would bear anything as long as she was learning.

One of the professors at La Maternité was a young doctor, Monsieur Hippolyte Blot. Shy with all the young women, he seemed especially shy with Elizabeth at first, though he did manage to say, "You know much about medicine, Mademoiselle." Elizabeth thought he was quite handsome. She wrote, "I think he must be...very much in awe of me, for he never ventures to give me a direct look, and seems so troubled when I address him."

Maybe Monsieur Blot was troubled because he found Elizabeth attractive. Soon the two of them began to be friends. One day, Monsieur Blot offered to lend her some medical journals. On another, he asked her to give him lessons in English. When she did, Monsieur Blot began helping her with French. One subject they talked and argued about, in both languages, was scientific experimentation on animals. Monsieur Blot believed it was all right to use animals to advance science. Elizabeth strongly disagreed. She thought it was cruel and unnecessary.

But even to disagree with Hippolyte Blot was pleasant. "This companionship was a great relief to my imprisonment in La Maternité...," wrote Elizabeth. After more time had gone by, she wrote, "I like him. I hope we may come a little more closely together." Slowly Elizabeth began to realize that she was in love with Monsieur Blot. But what good could ever come of this? Marrying him would mean giving up her own goals, for she could never be a surgeon in France. And she knew his family would be outraged if he married an American woman and, even worse, one who dared to claim she was a doctor herself!

One night Elizabeth was distracted from these thoughts when she was invited to watch a major operation, performed without anesthesia, which was still new and rarely used. Elizabeth, very disturbed by the pain suffered by the poor woman patient, vowed to use anesthesia when she became a surgeon. The filthy jacket the surgeon wore disgusted her and so did the dirty knife he used. An older student said to Elizabeth, "Surgeons are proud of all the dried blood on their jackets. It is like a badge of honor."

The day came when Elizabeth was allowed to leave La Maternité to visit Anna for eleven whole hours of vacation! "How gay and free and delightful the city seemed to me after my four months' imprisonment...I really saw Paris again for the first time."

But soon after her beautiful day with Anna, disaster overtook Elizabeth. She was treating a baby with the serious eye infection ophthalmia when some liquid from the baby's eye squirted into her own left eye. Her eye felt irritated all day and by the next morning it was frighteningly swollen. At last she went to Monsieur Blot and told him what had happened. "This is terrible, Mademoiselle! Such

The History of Anesthesia

In 1799, in England, Sir Humphry Davy noticed that pain was relieved when a patient breathed in nitrous oxide, a gas. He named it "laughing gas." His pupil, Michael Faraday, discovered that ether, a liquid, produced similar results when patients breathed in the vapor that ether gives off. But surgeons did not begin using anesthetics until 1842. In 1844, Horace Wells, a U.S. dentist, had one of his own teeth removed while he inhaled "laughing gas." In 1847, Sir James Y. Simpson used chloroform (another liquid which gives off vapor that patients breathe) to lessen childbirth pain. Queen Victoria was one of the first women to experience this anesthetic for childbirth and she greatly approved.

Today, many kinds of anesthesia are available. "General" anesthesia is the term for blocking pain by putting the patient to sleep. With "local" anesthesia, only a part of the body is numbed so no pain is felt.

infection can lead to blindness. We must treat this with every possible weapon."

Elizabeth was given a hospital bed. Hippolyte Blot gave up all his other work to care for her. Some of the treatments were very hard to bear: leeches sucking her forehead may have been the worst. Anna visited her three times a day, often crying at the sight of her sister.

Even frightened and in pain, Elizabeth was happy when Hippolyte was near her. "My friendly young doctor came every two hours, day and night, to tend the eye," she wrote. "My friendship deepened for my young physician." One night, when he thought she was asleep, Hippolyte spoke to her in a way that told Elizabeth he loved her. How she longed to tell him she loved him, too! It was very hard to force herself to say nothing. But she thought, *I will never let him know that I heard him, for I know my future must be medicine, not marriage.*

But how much sight would she have in that future? At the end of three weeks, Elizabeth still had no sight in her left eye. Was this to be the end of her ambition to be a surgeon? A surgeon must have very sharp eyesight.

OPHTHALMIA OF LITTLE DANGER NOW

➤ A contagious eye infection caused by bacteria, ophthalmia almost inevitably caused blindness in the past. Today, it is easily cleared up with antibiotics. Treatments used in Elizabeth's time were of little or no use. They included bleeding the patient, bathing the eye, injections of useless substances, cold compresses, a diet of nothing but broth, and even footbaths.

Beginning of Antiseptic Conditions in Medicine and Surgery

Until the late 1800s, most doctors did not understand the importance of antiseptic conditions (keeping out bacteria that cause infections) in medicine and surgery. They did not wash their hands, their instruments, or their clothing. Doctors themselves thus spread infection from patient to patient. Louis Pasteur was one of the first scientists to write that harmful bacteria or germs cause infections and to urge cleanliness. In 1865, Joseph Lister succeeded in preventing infection in wounds by treating them with carbolic acid, which destroyed bacteria, but the medical profession resisted accepting his methods.

In the 1800s, many women died of childbirth fever. In 1843, Oliver Wendell Holmes argued that doctors were infecting their patients and must wash their hands. Again, doctors refused to listen. In 1847, Ignaz Semmelweis discovered that doctors were infecting maternity patients by attending autopsies and then caring for patients without washing their hands, thus spreading germs and disease from dead bodies to new mothers. Doctors ridiculed his theory for years before it was finally accepted.

When she left La Maternité at the end of November, Elizabeth knew her friendship with Hippolyte Blot would never be more than that. Their lives must go in different directions. They parted with words of friendship. Elizabeth concealed the pain she felt at this separation from the man who had cared for her so tenderly and spoken to her of love.

She spent months at Anna's house in Paris, waiting for her left eye to improve. Though the eye did not get any better, one of her wishes did come true: a letter came from St. Bartholomew's hospital in London, admitting her for advanced medical training in any department she wished.

MEDICAL EXPERIMENTS ON ANIMALS

➤ Elizabeth always argued against the use of animals in medical experiments. Upset when she heard about an experiment on a dog, she wrote: "...conscience and humanity must guide...curiosity, or we wander from the highroad of truth into...error...the eager young student, thirsting for knowledge may be blind to unscientific or immoral methods."

➤ Today, people still disagree about whether it is right or necessary to use animals in medical research. Some believe such research is justified in order to help people. Others believe it is never right and that other ways can be found to do necessary medical research.

"I'll choose surgery, of course," Elizabeth said. Anna did not say anything. But a short time later, Elizabeth had to face the truth. She was blind in one eye and always would be. "Well, there is more than one branch of medicine," she said. "I have one good eye and with that eye I will look at my patients and see what I must do to help them."

Before long Elizabeth faced another truth. Her left eye had to be removed to prevent the infection in the bad eye from spreading to the good eye.

In August, Dr. Louis Desmarres, a well-known eye surgeon, removed her left eye and replaced it with a glass eye. Elizabeth was grateful that she looked almost normal after the surgery but much more grateful that her right eye was saved.

"How joyfully I leave Paris and go to England to study at St. Bartholomew's!" she wrote home.

CHAPTER 11

SUCCESS IN LONDON

All the medical students at St. Bartholomew's Hospital in London were invited to the home of James Paget, a famous surgeon, for breakfast before the new term began. Elizabeth, wondering how she would be treated as the only woman student, felt shy as she approached the Paget house.

"Welcome, Miss Blackwell, to London and to our Hospital," said Dr. Paget, as Elizabeth entered. "And this morning, my wife and I welcome you to our home, too."

Dr. Paget's welcome warmed her. She was tired of feeling strange and unwanted. Sipping her coffee in the comfortable dining room, answering the polite students who asked about her former training, Elizabeth relaxed. Maybe at St. Bartholomew's, she would finally be considered just another advanced medical student, one who knew a good deal about medicine and was eager to learn much more.

She did notice that Mrs. Paget, while kind, kept glancing at her with a shocked, puzzled look. *She never expected to have a female medical student in her home,* Elizabeth thought, smiling at the surgeon's wife. *To her, I am like a strange exhibit in her husband's laboratory.*

A few days later, Elizabeth attended a dinner party at the Paget home. That evening she sensed how different she was from the other women. She wore a plain gray wool dress with a high neckline. Mrs. Paget and her other women guests wore elegant silk dresses with elaborate necklaces glittering at the low necklines. They seemed amazed that she was actually a medical student. When Dr. Paget later said to her at the hospital, "You will find that women object to your career as a doctor more than men do," Elizabeth remembered the women guests at his dinner party and decided he was right, at least about women in England.

St. Bartholomew's Hospital, London. (Culver Pictures.)

But the men were respectful enough. When Elizabeth entered the room for Dr. Paget's first lecture of the term, the other students applauded her. Every day after that, she left her boarding house and walked to class with confidence, passing the Smithfield Cattle Market where the sounds of pigs and bulls mixed with the London street sounds of horses and carriages and shouting children. She knew Dr. Paget would reserve a seat for her at his lecture and that she would be treated as if she belonged.

More important to Elizabeth than the lectures were the patients. At La Maternité, she studied and treated new mothers and their babies. At St. Bartholomew's, she saw every kind of patient, every sickness. While feeling sympathy for the suffering patients, Elizabeth was grateful to have so many chances to learn and help. Although all the hospital wards were open to her, the doctor in charge of women's diseases was strongly opposed to women doctors. "I will not do anything to help educate you," he told Elizabeth. He added that he did not object to her personally. He would treat any other woman just the same! Elizabeth did not find this very comforting.

Other senior doctors were more helpful. Some asked her to come along on their visits to patients. Others explained their research projects to her. Some invited her on visits to other hospitals. She met Dr. Oldham of Guy's Hospital who said, "Women in medicine? What a splendid idea! And you say your sister will be a doctor, too? Send her to work with us here at Guy's when she's ready."

Busy as she was, Elizabeth had not forgotten Hippolyte

Blot. But before long he wrote her with the news of his engagement, then his marriage. In his letters he called her his "dear sister," and himself her brother. Elizabeth, missing him, was glad she had never spoken to him of love. This way they could go on being friends, at least in letters.

And there were new friendships to enjoy. At first Elizabeth was disappointed with the women she met; they all seemed interested mainly in clothes and needlework. But one day three young women called on her. "We've heard about you," they told her. "We wanted to meet the woman who is doing such interesting, exciting things. We believe in women's right to do whatever work they want to. You are changing the world!"

One of the young women, Barbara Leigh Smith, a painter, would become a close friend. Her father, like Elizabeth's, believed daughters should be educated and have the chance to use their knowledge and talents to do anything they wished. The other two women with Barbara that day were her sister, Nannie, and a friend, Bessie. Elizabeth's three new friends soon decorated her room with pictures and flowers. "You've made it look and feel like a home," the grateful Elizabeth said. She had lived for too long in bleak boarding-house rooms. Barbara even helped Elizabeth with gifts of money, though Elizabeth insisted that the money was a loan.

With friends who shared her interests, Elizabeth's life was now richer. At the end of a long day of lectures and hospital visits, she attended parties, plays or concerts. But, still concerned about money, on many a late night she would walk back to her boarding house. She would not hire a horse-drawn cab when she could perfectly well walk.

One day, Barbara introduced Elizabeth to her cousin, Florence Nightingale. Barbara said, "You are both interested in medicine, so I thought you should know each other."

"Do you want to be a doctor?" Elizabeth asked the beautiful, graceful girl with the thick brown hair. She could tell from Florence's elegant clothes that she, like Barbara, was the daughter of a wealthy family. *What do Florence's family think about her interest in medicine?* Elizabeth wondered.

That, it turned out, was Florence's problem. "I want to be a nurse," Florence said, "and to work in a hospital. My family is so upset they would almost rather I were dead. At least then I would not disgrace them."

Elizabeth was not surprised. Nurses were considered little better than servants. They were poorly trained and did more rough work, like scrubbing, than real medical care. Therefore, nursing was not thought to be respectable work and no well brought up young lady ever became a nurse. Elizabeth said slowly, "I know nurses do good work and are needed, but…it is a hard life for a lady."

Florence said, "I know what you're thinking. Nurses are uneducated girls. But nursing doesn't have to be like that — it should be a serious medical profession. Nurses should be well trained. I want to change everything about nursing. But my family won't even let me begin."

Elizabeth thought, *How lucky I was! My family encouraged me to do what I wanted.*

Florence invited Elizabeth to visit her family's grand country house. They spent long hours together, walking in the gardens, discussing their ideas about sickness and health. Florence said, "People must learn to be clean if they want to be healthy."

Florence Nightingale and the Nursing Profession

Florence overcame her family's objections to nursing when she was thirty-three and took charge of a nursing home. She began to improve the training of nurses when England went to war against Russia in 1854. Wounded English soldiers at the British hospital in Scutari, Turkey received little medical care.

The British Secretary of War, an old friend of Florence's, asked her to recruit and equip a group of nurses and take them to Scutari. Though the doctors resisted working with women, Florence organized her nurses into effective caregivers who reduced suffering and saved lives. Her work made her world-famous. After the war, Florence wrote books on nursing, on hospitals, and on home health care. She fulfilled her dream of transforming the training of nurses when the Nightingale School for nurses opened in 1860. In 1907, she was named "a pioneer of the Red Cross Movement."

Elizabeth nodded. "And they need fresh air and exercise."

"We have the same beliefs about health," Florence said. Pointing to her family's large house, she added, "Don't you think this house would make a wonderful hospital? If only we could turn it into one and work in it together, Elizabeth, I would be so happy. That would be such a useful life."

Elizabeth's thoughts, though, were turning in another direction. "It is time I started practicing medicine," she said. "But I want to go back to America. That's where women will first be treated as equal to men, so it's where I can best make a contribution to medicine."

Elizabeth was thinking of her family, too. Her mother was in America, and most of her sisters and brothers. And there was the dream of practicing medicine together with Emily. Yes, it was time to go home.

"I shall become a nurse," Florence said with great determination.

"I shall be a doctor in America," Elizabeth said. And so the two friends parted.

12

STRUGGLING TO SUCCEED IN NEW YORK

Mama, Marian, and Ellen welcomed Elizabeth at the dock in New York. They hoped to take her back with them to the family home in Cincinnati, but Elizabeth said, "I must start my medical practice here in New York."

Elizabeth's heart was warmed by her family's welcome. But before long her experiences made her feel anything but welcomed by New Yorkers. When she tried to rent rooms to practice medicine, landladies were quick to turn her away. "A woman doctor! Not in my house! I run a respectable home, Miss." Elizabeth had not been treated with so much distrust since her early days at medical school in Geneva. Once again people thought she was crazy or had bad morals or was planning to practice some evil trade. *You would think I was a witch, or worse*, Elizabeth said to herself.

But soon she faced rejections that hurt much more. She visited hospitals and clinics, introduced herself, and explained her training and experience. The reaction was always the same: "No, madam, we cannot admit you to our staff. We have no need of a female physician."

I am thirty years old, she thought, *and I must begin my life's work, but how can I?* It was late summer, the heat hard to bear, as she walked the streets looking for a place to rent or a hospital that would hire her.

Finally, Elizabeth managed to rent an entire floor of a house in Greenwich Village, the neighborhood her family lived in when they first arrived in the United States. The rent for so much space was more than she could afford, but it was the only place that would accept her. Even then, the landlady complained that the sign reading "Elizabeth Blackwell, M.D." was shocking enough to keep other tenants away.

Rats swarm over sleeping patients in Bellevue Hospital, New York City, 1860s. (Culver Pictures.)

Elizabeth bought medical supplies to equip a simple office. So the sign was displayed, the office was ready, and a well-trained doctor was eager for work. Horace Greeley, editor and publisher of the *New York Tribune,* liked the idea of women doctors and was willing to help. He published an announcement in his newspaper that Elizabeth Blackwell, M.D. had opened an office. But where were the patients? They did not come and it seemed as if they never would. Greeley even published a little article a few weeks later mentioning Elizabeth's office address again and claiming she was already successful in her practice. Still no patients.

While she wandered the city searching for rooms and visiting hospitals, Elizabeth had noticed how unhealthy many New York children looked. "I have thought of something useful to do while I wait for patients to accept me," Elizabeth wrote to Emily. "I will write and lecture on health." She decided to concentrate on girls' health. Alone in her medical office, she began to write down her thoughts on what girls should be taught about healthy living and about their own bodies.

As she wrote, Elizabeth remembered her lively conversations with Florence Nightingale in England. Their shared belief in exercise, sports, fresh air, and good food found their way into her writing. But writing was only half the battle. Elizabeth knew she had to conquer her shyness and begin to lecture to the public.

She placed an announcement in the newspaper stating that Dr. Elizabeth Blackwell would give six lectures in a church basement; tickets could be bought for two dollars at a bookstore. *Will anyone come?* she asked herself. *If they come, will they disagree? How will they act?*

She was shaking with fear as she began her first lecture, to an audience of just a few women. Many of them were Quakers, members of a religious group called the Society of Friends. "Let your daughters take part in active sports," Elizabeth told them. "Let them wear loose, comfortable clothes. Encourage them to feel they can do useful work in the world." Her voice grew stronger as she relaxed and became used to speaking.

"I was shocked at some things you said, Dr. Blackwell," one woman said after a lecture and many other women said the same. Elizabeth had talked about sex and birth and told her listeners that teenage girls should be given information about these topics. These were very new ideas at a time when even the word "body" was shocking!

"We *knew* a woman doctor was up to no good!" was one reaction to Elizabeth's lectures. She was even jeered at by a crowd in the street for the topics she dared to mention. *Well, life is hard but I can bear hard things,* she thought.

But at least Elizabeth no longer waited alone in her office. A few women patients came and, in time, a few more. "I believe you can care for me as well as any man," said a woman who attended the lectures. Soon there were whole families who considered Elizabeth the family doctor.

One year after Elizabeth returned to New York from England, Emily arrived from Cincinnati. "I'm so happy to see you again," said Elizabeth to the younger sister who wanted to be a doctor. She thought, *It's been four years. I hardly know her any more. Is she strong enough to stand the rejection that will surely come her way?*

Sure enough, rejections began to pour in from the medical schools Emily applied to. "Hasn't anything changed since you did this?" Emily asked Elizabeth.

"Change is slow," Elizabeth answered. "But I know it does come."

A day came when both sisters had reason to celebrate. "I had three patients this week," Elizabeth said, greeting Emily after work. Three patients were the most she had ever treated in one week.

Emily was waving a letter. "And I've been admitted to Rush Medical College in Chicago!"

"That's the best news of all!" Elizabeth cried. "We'll be partners before long."

Emily was off to Chicago, leaving Elizabeth still with too few patients. She longed to treat poor patients in a clinic, a medical office where they paid nothing or whatever they could afford. But no clinic would hire her. *I will start my own clinic,* she decided. She rented a room in a slum neighborhood where no other medical care was available. A slaughterhouse was nearby and pigs roamed the streets, a source of filth and smells. Soon Elizabeth's sign brought results. Poor women timidly climbed the stairs to seek help from the lady doctor. Most were foreign-born and spoke little or no English. Elizabeth treated them for free, though sometimes the pride of the poorest women led them to offer her a few pennies. Some of Elizabeth's Quaker friends donated money to help with the rent and supplies.

Elizabeth offered free medical care to poor residents of crowded New York City streets such as this one. (Culver Pictures.)

Elizabeth's patients received more than free treatment. As always, she believed education for healthy living was even more important than treating disease. "You must keep your children clean and take them out into the fresh air and sunlight and keep the flies away from their food," she told the mothers who came to her clinic. Many did not understand or were too overworked and had too many children to do a better job of caring for them. But many neighborhood families brought up healthier children because of Elizabeth's good advice.

Late one night, a child knocked on Elizabeth's door. "Please come, doctor, my mother needs you!" he cried. Elizabeth followed him up five flights of stairs in a rundown house in a narrow street. There she found his mother in labor, lying on the floor on a heap of rags.

It was a long night. In the morning, when Elizabeth left, the new baby was in its mother's arms and the whole family was grateful to the doctor.

There were many nights like that one. Each time, as Elizabeth walked home, she enjoyed the satisfaction of knowing that people who had no one else to care for them were safer because she was there.

13

"A CHILD WILL HAVE A PLACE IN MY HEART"

When Elizabeth walked the streets of New York longing to help children living in poverty, did she ever imagine one of them becoming her own child? When she treated mothers poor in money but rich in children did she ever envy them? In any case, in 1854 when she was thirty-three, she announced to her sister Marian, "I am going to adopt a child."

"Why, Elizabeth, what place could a child have in your life?"

"She will have a place in my home so I won't be lonely, and a place in my heart because I will love her."

"*She?* Well, at least a girl will be useful. She can be trained to help keep house. Many families take in orphan girls to help with the housework."

Elizabeth thought, *That's all right for others, but I want a companion, not a maid.*

She and Marian took the ferry over to Randall's Island, to a nursery where four hundred orphan immigrant children lived. Anyone who looked respectable could choose one and take that child home.

The children were all sizes, of different races, and many states of health. Elizabeth walked among them, smiling gently at each child, and looking them over carefully. Both Marian and the matron, the woman in charge of the children, expected Elizabeth to use her medical expertise to identify the strongest, healthiest girl and choose her. But Elizabeth kept coming back to a small, thin, delicate-looking little girl with wild black hair.

Marian drew her sister aside. "You can't be thinking of that one! Her eyes must be weak, for she blinks all the time. And her legs look wobbly as a new calf's."

The matron, who was listening, added: "In my opinion, she is a stupid child, too. You would do better to choose almost any other."

Elizabeth said, "She is the child who needs me most."

Her name was Kitty Barry, the matron said. She had come from Ireland and was probably seven or eight, though no one knew for sure. When Elizabeth said to her, "Would you like to come home with me and be my child?" Kitty answered, "Yes, and we'll always take care of each other."

Marian laughed at the notion that a weak, uneducated girl could do much taking care of strong, brilliant Elizabeth! But Kitty took care of Elizabeth by transforming her into a much loved, happy woman with her own child to enjoy and bring up.

Why did Kitty seem weak and stupid? Only because no one had given her the care she needed. When Elizabeth taught her, she learned fast. The gymnastic exercises Elizabeth gave her to do soon strengthened her legs.

She did help with the housekeeping, but only as any daughter would. And Elizabeth, who in the past had rushed from work to home without a pause, now lingered in toyshops, choosing gifts for her Kitty.

One Sunday found Elizabeth and Kitty on the ferry to Staten Island, for a picnic in the country. Anyone who saw the short woman with wavy blond hair and the small black-haired child laughing and talking together that day would have understood that they were indeed taking good care of each other! They might, though, have been surprised to hear the child addressing the woman as "Doctor" or "My Doctor" for that is what Kitty liked to call Elizabeth.

Kitty was puzzled one day when a male physician friend of Elizabeth's came to tea. "I never knew a man could be a doctor!" she said when he had gone.

On another day, Kitty answered the door and ran to find Elizabeth, saying, "There's a lady downstairs but I can't understand her." Elizabeth did not understand the lady either at first, for she spoke in Polish, but they soon realized that they both spoke German.

"My name is Marie Zakrzewska," the newcomer said. "I am a midwife but I want to become a doctor. I have heard that you can help me perhaps." Elizabeth discovered that Marie had been the head midwife and a professor at a large hospital in Germany.

"I need an assistant in my clinic," Elizabeth said. "We can work together while you learn English and then I'll help you get into medical school."

Marie's name was pronounced *Zak-shef-ska* but Kitty dubbed her "Dr. Zak". Because she knew even more about childbirth than Elizabeth did she was a most valuable assistant. When Marie's English became good enough, Elizabeth kept her promise and helped her enter Cleveland Medical College.

Elizabeth wrote to Emily, "It is time for women doctors to open their own hospital. You and I will be the doctors who do it. And Dr. Zak will be the third. Together we will open a new world in medicine."

ADOPTING A CHILD TODAY

➤ Now adoptive parents are investigated by social workers who make certain they are moral, dependable, healthy people who are able to support a child and bring it up properly. All adoptions must also be approved by a judge. In the recent past, only married couples could adopt. Today, single people are often allowed to adopt. Most parents wish to adopt newborn infants, although there are many older children who need homes, as Kitty Barry did. Some U.S. citizens travel to foreign countries to adopt infants. In one recent ten-year period, about 130,000 adoptions took place in the United States each year.

14

TURNING AN OLD HOUSE INTO A NEW HOSPITAL

Elizabeth bought a house on Fifteenth Street. Because she could not really afford it, she rented most of the house and kept only one downstairs room for a medical office, plus the attic for herself and Kitty to live in.

That it was her own house brought her special satisfaction when she and Emily and Marie were ready to practice medicine together. The three boldly hung their signs out front. "Now there's no landlady to complain that women doctors will disgrace the house," Elizabeth said.

But life was moving fast. The three women already had plans that went far beyond their own house for the practice of medicine. They were deeply involved in Elizabeth's grand ambition to open a hospital for women.

"Money," Elizabeth said, sighing. "There is always the question of where the money is to come from."

"But think of all the women we know who want to help us," Emily said. "They are knitting and sewing all day long and planning to sell everything they make for the benefit of the hospital."

"Oh, that!" Marie scoffed. "They talk of nothing but this Fair where they will sell the things. But you can't finance a hospital with baby booties! We will need furniture and supplies and equipment. And what of the building itself?"

Elizabeth said, "The Fair will raise some money and every bit is important. But I have other methods in mind, too."

Elizabeth gave lectures in New York to raise money. She lectured in private houses, at Sunday schools, at meetings of all sorts of groups. When her listeners were politely asked to pledge money for the hospital, they often asked, "Why must there be a hospital run by and for women?"

Elizabeth answered: "Though there are now a few women doctors, hospitals still refuse to admit them for further training with patients. A women's hospital will be a place for new women doctors to complete their education. And it will serve poor women who cannot afford care anywhere else." Elizabeth did not raise much money in New York, for the city's residents often expressed horror at the shocking notion of women being completely in charge of a *hospital*!

Marie had more success. She traveled to Boston, where many people were more open to new ideas. She went directly to wealthy people she knew and to their friends, asking for money. Slowly the hospital fund grew.

For a while it seemed that the Fair, for which all that knitting and sewing had been going on, would never have a home. No one wanted to rent a space to women. Finally, a friend of Elizabeth's found them an ugly, fourth floor loft with unfinished floors and walls. Quickly, the women borrowed rugs, pictures, and even a chandelier to make it attractive.

The Fair ran for four days. Horace Greeley, Elizabeth's friend at the *New York Tribune,* wrote an article about the Fair for his newspaper. This time Greeley's publicity was a

Hygiene And Life Expectancy

Life expectancy in the United States increased dramatically during the twentieth century, from only 47.3 years in 1900, to 75.7 years by 1994, an increase of about two-thirds. According to a report published in *Population and Development Review* in September 1998, life spans had never before increased so much. Though it was well known that death rates dropped during the twentieth century, this report makes it clear that most of the change occurred during the first half of the century and that most of the advances in health were due not to advanced medical treatments, but to improvements in sanitation and public health. Once they realized that germs cause disease, people also realized the importance of clean water, clean food, handwashing, and keeping sick people away from healthy people.

big help. People streamed up the stairs, gladly paying the ten cents admission. Shoppers, mostly women, crowded the aisles between the display tables, admiring the embroidered tablecloths, the crocheted shawls and baby blankets, the painted china — and not just admiring but buying. Friends of Emily's in England had sent all sorts of crafts and trinkets that sold quickly at an "English table." Of course, the Fair, three weeks before Christmas, was perfectly timed for gift-buying!

When the Fair was over, Elizabeth, Emily, and Marie had just enough money for their hospital. They bought an old house on Bleecker Street and began to transform it. The living room, dining room, and study became wards with beds for patients. So did two bedrooms on the second floor. One day, Elizabeth startled a workman by demanding he install a huge window in a small bedroom. "Why would you be wanting a big window when you'll just be sleeping under it in the dark night?" the man asked.

"The room we're standing in will be an operating room," Elizabeth explained, "and our surgeons will need light."

The third floor was turned into the maternity ward. The attic became the living space for resident doctors and medical students.

Friends donated furniture. Elizabeth's was probably the first hospital furnished partly with antique velvet chairs and satin sofas. The women added curtains, pictures, and plants to create a warm atmosphere. Medical instruments were arranged on shaky old tables and stands. Druggists donated medicines. At last, everything was ready.

Elizabeth, Marie, and Emily walked through the building, imagining the wards filled with patients. Exciting as this was, Elizabeth was already planning ahead. "We will have more than a hospital one day," she said. "We'll also have a nursing school and a school to train women physicians."

While Elizabeth was busy getting the hospital ready, Kitty was not neglected. Elizabeth's mother had moved in with them and was having a wonderful time caring for her adopted granddaughter. Kitty, in turn, enjoyed her new big family, for uncles and aunts were constantly arriving for visits. Kitty was doing well at the 12th Street Public School for Girls, known as the best school in the city.

The New York Infirmary for Indigent Women and Children opened on May 12, 1857. Elizabeth had chosen Florence Nightingale's birthday for the opening, to honor her old friend.

And patients came, first former clinic patients, then new patients as word spread. Four medical students soon moved in to spend the summer between their school terms. When two nurses in training joined the hospital, the New York Infirmary became the first American nursing school.

The workload of the three doctors was very heavy because they had to do everything. They not only treated hospital patients and private office patients but also had to make up menus for patients' meals, go to the markets for food, shop for medicines and supplies, balance the accounts, and teach the students. In the evenings, the doctors even cut and sewed towels and pillowcases while listening to the students recite their lessons!

As if all that work wasn't enough, they also had to cope with fierce opposition to women running a hospital. Elizabeth didn't realize just how fierce until the day one of the maternity patients died of childbirth fever, despite the excellent sanitary and antiseptic conditions of the new hospital. Her relatives had known she was dangerously ill, but that didn't stop them from rioting outside the hospital. "They're throwing stones!" Emily cried, cringing as a shower of rocks hit the front windows. The patients and staff were terrified.

Elizabeth opened the outside door to see a crowd armed with shovels and iron tools moving toward the house. She heard shouts of "Female doctors are killers!" She remembered the Bristol riots in her childhood and how her father had risked his life holding back an angry crowd. Now it was her turn for action but she did not know what she could do.

Suddenly, a loud Irish male voice was heard above the crowd. "Listen, you fools! It's not the doctors' fault a woman died. These doctors cured my wife of pneumonia. But they're doctors, not God! Some sick people die and that's how it is."

The crowd's roar died down into grumbling. Soon they moved away from the hospital, weapons lowered.

Another dangerous crowd gathered when a patient died of a ruptured appendix. This time, a male doctor who was consulting at the hospital invited twelve of the patients' male relatives to attend the autopsy. "You will see for yourselves the terrible effect this illness had on this woman's body," the doctor said.

They saw, and they agreed that the women doctors were not at fault. Elizabeth said to them, "I understand your anger. I know that we women doctors have to prove ourselves all the time."

Except for these events, the hospital was quietly succeeding, both in healing its patients and training doctors and nurses. And Elizabeth's basic philosophy of health had not been forgotten. "People *must* keep clean, sick people and well people both," the staff and students continually reminded everyone, hospital patients, clinic patients, and patients' families. They gave out soap along with medicines.

A LASTING LEGACY

➤ By the late 1920s, the hospital Elizabeth founded employed forty-five female doctors and was staffed entirely by women. Although it moved to different buildings over the years, the hospital is still caring for patients today. Called the New York Infirmary-Beekman Downtown Hospital for many years, it is now known as New York University Downtown Hospital and is part of the New York University Medical Center. An oil painting of Elizabeth hangs in the hospital lobby along with a painting of Emily. Down the hall is a mural illustrating one of the early buildings of Elizabeth's hospital, on its busy New York square.

While Elizabeth and Emily were deeply involved with their hospital, their brothers Henry and Sam were involved in major issues of the day: the abolition of slavery and women's rights.

Henry fell in love with Lucy Stone, a leader in the fight for increased rights for women. Lucy claimed marriage would interfere with her work. One day, in early 1855, Henry entered a train compartment in the North where a slave child was traveling with her owners. He asked the girl if she wanted to be free, and when she said yes he took her off the train. He was then charged with kidnapping. The charges were dropped when the judge decided slaves were free if their owners took them into free territory. Lucy was

Mural showing an early building of the hospital Elizabeth founded. (Courtesy, NYU Downtown Hospital.)

so impressed with his bravery that she agreed to marry him. Together they were tireless workers for women's rights for the rest of their lives, as was their daughter, Alice Stone Blackwell.

In January 1856, Sam married Antoinette Brown, the first woman in America to become an ordained minister. They had five daughters; two became doctors. The tradition of strong women in the Blackwell family remained an enduring one.

15

TRAINING NURSES FOR THE CIVIL WAR

In 1860, Abraham Lincoln was elected President. The conflict between the North and the South over slavery became more and more heated. Lincoln declared that slavery must not be tolerated in any part of the United States. On April 12, 1861, the Civil War began.

To Elizabeth, war meant one thing: wounded soldiers must be cared for. "Our work now is to train nurses for the war," she told Emily. She thought about the vitally important work Florence Nightingale had done during wartime. Now it was her turn.

The first task was to choose those women likely to make good nurses. They had to be intelligent enough to learn medical and nursing skills, dedicated enough to stand the sights and smells of the battlefield, and tender enough to be a comfort to soldiers suffering fear and pain. Elizabeth thought back to her days as a student at La Maternité. What qualities had made the best nurses good at their work? When she interviewed the women who volunteered to be trained as nurses, she imagined them at La Maternité. No, she might think about one woman, you are too much like the nurses who were careless or ignorant or who laughed at a patient's pain. Or yes, you seem smart and tough and kind, you will do admirably.

The women Elizabeth selected attended her Infirmary for one month's instruction, then went on to another New York hospital for another month of training. Before the war, nurses training at the Infirmary studied for thirteen months. "How can we teach them enough in only two months?" Emily asked, nearly despairing at the task ahead.

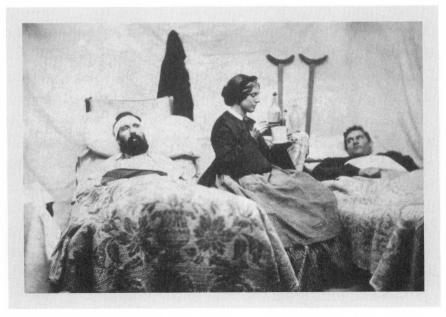

Nurse Anne Bell cares for two wounded northern soldiers during the Civil War. (Corbis.)

Elizabeth said calmly, "The answer is the same as it often is in medicine: we do the best we can."

After the brief training period, the women traveled to Washington, D.C., where the Superintendent of Nurses sent them to the war zones. By January 1862, Elizabeth had sent fifty nurses to Washington.

Although New York was far from the fighting, all was not calm. Many Northerners believed in slavery and opposed abolition. They were furious that the North, their own home territory, was fighting the South.

Riots broke out in the streets of the city. Again Elizabeth thought of the Bristol riots of her childhood. Would people always use violence to settle their differences? Once more armed mobs surged forward like tidal waves, shouting, threatening. The noise of breaking glass filled her ears and the sky nearby blazed red. A dozen houses close to the Infirmary had been set on fire; window glass shattered from the flames.

The Blackwells, already unpopular with many people who thought women should not be doctors or run hospitals, were also known to be strongly in favor of abolition. The Infirmary also had black maternity patients, refugees from the South. For all these reasons they were in danger. Would the Infirmary be invaded? Elizabeth moved from ward to ward, trying to reassure her terrified patients, black and white.

"We'll be killed!" one woman cried.

"What will happen to my baby?" another whimpered.

"God is protecting us," Elizabeth said.

That night, a black woman who had escaped from slavery gave birth to her baby, born into freedom in the Infirmary.

The rioting continued for three days. Somehow Elizabeth's hospital and everyone in it escaped harm.

Then trouble erupted within the Infirmary itself. Some of Elizabeth's nurses protested her policy of admitting white war refugees from the South as patients. "Our soldiers are fighting against these Southerners! Why should we try to heal them?" they demanded.

"In this hospital, we care for the sick no matter what side they represent," Elizabeth said. "We are medical people and have no right to judge our patients."

In June 1864, with the war still on, Elizabeth's service to her country in training nurses was recognized. She was invited to go to Washington to inspect the Nursing Corps. On the way, traveling through Maryland where slavery had already been abolished, she rejoiced that all the black people she saw were free.

Elizabeth was invited to meet the President. Lincoln was relaxed and friendly. He and Elizabeth discussed the war. She wrote to Kitty that the President was much homelier than his photographs but that he must be very intelligent.

Elizabeth grieved with the rest of the country when the President was assassinated on April 14, 1865. She always remembered the tall smiling man who greeted her so warmly, sat on the edge of his desk, and talked to her as if there was nothing unusual about a serious discussion with a woman.

A month later, on May 26, the war ended with the sur-render of the last Confederate army at Shreveport, Louisiana.

Elizabeth and Emily talked of the changes the war had brought. Besides the end of slavery, there were welcome dif-ferences in women's lives. Elizabeth said, "Women are freer now than they were. They've shown how important their contribution is. We can work, and lead organizations, and raise money, and we can still be ladies."

"Women did all that even before the war," Emily said.

"That's true," Elizabeth said, "but the war brought many things to public notice. Our nurses were truly appreciated by soldiers and their families. Newspapers told the whole country how important nurses and other women were to the war effort." She added, "Now we women at the New York Infirmary will put our efforts into our next project."

16

THIS MEDICAL COLLEGE IS FOR WOMEN

Elizabeth knew that the hospital she had founded was only one step on the road of improved medicine. She had long dreamed of starting a medical school for women, partly because she disapproved of the low educational standards of all medical schools. Many schools required only ten months of classes and no practical experience with patients at all. Elizabeth fumed. How could such graduates be considered doctors? She would certainly not let them anywhere near a patient of hers!

Elizabeth not only dreamed of her medical school. She worked for years to raise money for it. At last, there was enough to finance a first-class medical college to train first-class women doctors.

In November 1868, the Woman's Medical College of the New York Infirmary opened its doors. In her speech at the official opening, Elizabeth said that while it was important to be sympathetic to sick people, it was knowledge that made good medicine, knowledge that made patients well.

At this new medical school, students were admitted only after they passed entrance examinations. They attended classes for three years, with a longer school year than other medical schools. They learned medicine by observing actual patients at the Infirmary as well as from the lectures of their instructors.

The first class consisted of seventeen women students, with eleven professors and instructors. Naturally, Elizabeth

A student dissects the leg of a cadaver at the Woman's Medical College, New York City, c. 1870. (Corbis / Bettmann.)

First graduates of the Woman's Medical College receive their diplomas, 1873. (Corbis / Bettmann.)

herself was the Professor of Hygiene. "Living in a clean environment prevents sickness," she told every student, for they were all required to take this course. "It is better to prevent sickness than to try to cure it."

Emily was Professor of Obstetrics and Women's Diseases. Several well-known men doctors also served on the faculty. One of them was Dr. Stephen Smith, who had been a classmate of Elizabeth's at Geneva College.

Curious visitors often came to stare at the strange sight of *women* students calmly dissecting bodies. The women

Elizabeth's Mistake

Elizabeth never believed it was necessary or desirable for doctors to vaccinate people to prevent disease. She believed too completely in the power of hygiene and good sanitation to prevent disease. Because bacteria and viruses can cause disease even in people who live the most healthful lives, in the cleanest conditions, vaccination is necessary to prevent illness in individuals and to prevent epidemics of illness in large population groups.

wore big aprons over their full skirts and tied back their hair with scarves. A magazine article of the time reported: "The education is equal to that of any school in the country."

With the College safely established, Elizabeth felt her major work was done. In 1869, she moved back to England with Kitty. Mother and daughter lived together in great harmony, always with a much-loved dog for company. Elizabeth wrote books on health and on bringing up children, with Kitty helping as her secretary.

With Kitty beside her, Elizabeth died peacefully at Kilmun, a favorite place in Scotland, in 1910. At her death, she was eighty-nine years old, a pioneer in medicine, in healthful living, in education, and in furthering women's place in the world.

MEDICAL EDUCATION TODAY

➤ In the United States medical schools admit only college graduates who have also scored well on special medical school admission tests. During the first two years of a four-year course of study, students attend classes in all systems of the human body. During the final two years, students train by observing, diagnosing, and helping to treat patients in clinics and hospitals. After they receive the degree of Doctor of Medicine they must still undergo further training.

➤ They work in hospitals for one or two years as "interns," treating patients under the supervision of fully trained doctors. Those wishing to become specialists in some field of medicine (for example, surgery or women's or children's health) train for about three more years, working with patients and studying with doctors who are specialists in that field.

HONORING ELIZABETH

➤ Fifty years after Elizabeth graduated from Geneva College, the school named a dormitory in her honor. Fifty years after that, the school (now called Hobart College) celebrated the one hundredth anniversary of Elizabeth's graduation by honoring twelve distinguished women physicians for their achievements in medicine. In 1958, Hobart College inaugurated an annual Elizabeth Blackwell Award, given to a person who has performed "outstanding service to mankind." The U.S. government recently issued an eighteen-cent postage stamp in honor of Elizabeth, with the inscription "Elizabeth Blackwell First Woman Physician."

The hospital Elizabeth founded has grown into this large modern building in downtown New York City. (Courtesy, NYU Downtown Hospital.)

CONTINUING WHAT ELIZABETH BLACKWELL STARTED

As the years go by, more and more women are becoming doctors, and medical researchers. Additionally, increased attention is being paid to the distinct medical needs of all women. In 1985, the U.S. Public Health Service reported a lack of research statistics on women and too little understanding of women's general health needs. Today, many research projects are directed at discovering the cause and cure of illnesses mainly affecting women, such as breast cancer and osteoporosis (brittle bones). Until recently, testing of new drugs and other treatments was done almost entirely on men, but today women are included in many studies. This is important since women usually weigh less than men and have a different body chemistry; therefore, their bodies may react differently. When women astronauts are included on space crews, the effects of space travel on women's bodies can be studied.

The women's movement of the last thirty years or so has resulted in women taking more responsibility for their own health and demanding to be included in decisions that affect them. With the help of such groundbreaking books as *Our Bodies, Ourselves,* published in 1969, women began to learn more about the natural functions of their own bodies, about childbirth, and about their health needs. Childbirth education classes result in women making personal decisions about labor, delivery, and breastfeeding. Women can now choose to have family members present when they give birth.

Though much has been done to insure healthier lives for women, much remains to be done. Research in preventing and treating many diseases and conditions is still needed. Each new drug must be tested on women. More research needs to be done on how women's health affects the physical and mental health of children and all family members. There are a vast number of opportunities for future physicians and researchers to improve the health, not only of women, but of all people.

It has been many years since medicine was only a man's world. If she were alive today, Elizabeth Blackwell would be deeply gratified but probably she would not be surprised.

TIMELINES

The World During Elizabeth's Life

1800s   The Industrial Revolution, begun in the 1700s, is extended by many inventions in the 1800s. By 1850, precision tools begin to make mass production and assembly line production possible.

1821   By Elizabeth's birth date, there are one and one-half million slaves in the United States.

1822   Louis Pasteur, pioneer in the study of disease, is born in France.

1820s–1840s Michael Faraday, a British scientist, makes many discoveries involving chemicals, electromagnetism, and electricity.

1825   City streets are lit by gaslamps by this year.

1829   First steam locomotive runs in the United States.

1833   All slaves in the British empire are freed; laws regulating child labor are passed in England.

1837–1901   Queen Victoria reigns in England.

1844   Samuel Morse sends the first message over a telegraph line.

1840s   These are years of hardship and food shortages in much of Europe. Revolutions in many countries (Italy, France, Germany, Austria, Hungary), especially in 1848, lead to the beginning of the end of monarchs as absolute rulers and to the rise of democracy.

1859   Charles Darwin publishes *The Origin of Species,* on the theory of evolution.

1860   Abraham Lincoln is elected President of the United States.

1861	The Civil War begins.
1865	The Civil War ends.
1867	Rebecca Cole, an African-American woman, graduates from Women's Medical College in Philadelphia.
1876	Alexander Graham Bell sends the first telephone message.
1880s	Rapid development of modern surgery takes place.
1885	Louis Pasteur cures rabies; the internal combustion engine to power cars is invented.
1889	Susan LaFlesche Picotte becomes the first American-Indian woman to receive an M.D.; electric elevators make U.S. skyscrapers possible.
1895	W. Roentgen discovers x-rays.
1898	Marie and Pierre Curie discover radium.
1903	The Wright brothers' first airplane takes off at Kitty Hawk, North Carolina.

Elizabeth's Life

1821	Elizabeth Blackwell is born in Bristol, England on February 3, the daughter of Samuel and Hannah Lane Blackwell.
1832	The Blackwell family moves to New York City.
1838	The family moves to Cincinnati, Ohio in May; Papa dies in August; the family starts a boarding school.
1844	Elizabeth moves to Henderson, Kentucky to teach in a girls' school.
1845	After deciding to become a doctor, she goes to Asheville, North Carolina to teach music and begin private medical study.
1847	Elizabeth moves to Philadelphia, Pennsylvania; applies to 29 medical schools; begins medical school at Geneva Medical College on November 7.

1848	During the summer between medical school terms, Elizabeth works in women's ward at Blockley Almshouse in Philadelphia.
1849	Elizabeth graduates from Geneva first in her class; studies as a midwife trainee at La Maternité in Paris; works with and falls in love with Dr. Hippolyte Blot; loses left eye due to disease caught from infant patient.
1850	In London, Elizabeth becomes an intern at St. Bartholomew's Hospital; Florence Nightingale becomes a friend.
1851	After moving back to New York to practice medicine, Elizabeth fails to attract patients.
1852	Elizabeth gives lectures on health emphasizing the proper care and education of girls; some women and families become patients.
1853	Elizabeth opens a clinic to offer free treatment to poor women and children.
1854	Kitty Barry, an Irish orphan, becomes Elizabeth's adopted daughter; Marie Zakrzewska arrives to help in Elizabeth's medical practice.
1857	Elizabeth opens the New York Infirmary for Indigent Women and Children on May 12.
1861	The New York Infirmary begins training nurses for the Civil War.
1864	In Washington, D.C., Elizabeth meets President Abraham Lincoln.
1868	Elizabeth opens the Woman's Medical College of the New York Infirmary, the first medical school for women.
1869	With Kitty, Elizabeth moves back to England.
1910	Elizabeth dies in Scotland on May 31, age 89.

RESOURCES

Bibliography:

Baker, Rachel. *The First Woman Doctor.* Messner, New York, 1944.

Brown, Jordan. *Elizabeth Blackwell.* American Woman of Achievement Series, Chelsea House, New York, 1989.

Clapp, Patricia. *Dr. Elizabeth: The Story of the First Woman Doctor.* Lothrap, Lee & Shepard, New York, 1974.

Grant, Matthew G., *Elizabeth Blackwell, Pioneer Doctor.* Gallery of Great Americans Series, Creative Education, Mankato, MN, 1974.

Kline, Nancy. *Elizabeth Blackwell, A Doctor's Triumph.* Barnard Biography Series, Conari, Berkeley, CA, 1997.

Klingel, Cindy. *Elizabeth Blackwell.* We The People Series, Creative Education, Mankato, MN, 1988.

Wilson, Dorothy Clarke. *Lone Woman, The Story of Elizabeth Blackwell The First Woman Doctor.* Little Brown, Boston, MA, 1970.

Web sites:

http://infoplease.lycos.com/bio/2-3eblackwell.html
http://hws.edu/NEW/bwaward/history.html
http://www.hws.edu/HIS/blackwell.html

INDEX

Page numbers in italics refer to photographs or drawings.